Funky Business

TALENT MAKES CAPITAL DANCE

K. Nordström
J. Ridderstråle

Pearson Education Limited

Head Office:
Edinburgh Gate
Harlow CM20 2JE
Tel: +44 (0)1279 623623
Fax: +44 (0)1279 431059

London Office:
128 Long Acre
London WC2E 9AN
Tel: +44 (0)207 447 2000
Fax: +44 (0)207 240 5771

Website: www.business-minds.com

First published in Great Britain in 2000
Published in Sweden in 1999 by
BookHouse Publishing AB

© BookHouse Publishing AB 2000

The right of Kjell A. Nordström and Jonas Ridderstråle to be
identified as authors of this work has been asserted by them in
accordance with the Copyright, Designs and Patents Act 1988.

ISBN 0 273 64591 9

British Library Cataloguing in Publication Data
A CIP catalogue record for this book can be obtained from the British Library.

10 9 8 7 6 5 4

Typeset by Pantek Arts, Maidstone, Kent
Printed and bound in Great Britain by Biddles Ltd, Guildford and King's Lynn

The Publishers' policy is to use paper manufactured from sustainable forests.

About the authors

FUNKSTER NO 1: Kjell A. Nordström

Kjell A. Nordström is based at the Institute of International Business at the Stockholm School of Economics where he received his PhD before running the School's International Business course and helping to found the prestigious Advanced Management Program. Kjell's research has focused on internationalization, and his experience is highly international with teaching engagements in China, Europe and North America. Forget dry theories, Kjell's ideas work. He makes things happen. In the real world, Kjell is on the board of directors of the highly internationalized Norwegian firm Stokke Fabrikker, Swedish Internet company Spray Ventures, and the US digital change agent Razorfish. He has also advised and acted as a consultant to many other organizations across the globe.

FUNKSTER NO 2: Jonas Ridderstråle

Based at the Centre for Advanced Studies in Leadership at the Stockholm School of Economics, Jonas Ridderstråle is at the forefront of the new generation of European-based business gurus. Jonas has an MBA and a doctorate from the Stockholm School of Economics and is the author of a book on global innovation. He has run the Advanced Management Program at the Stockholm School of Economics and has taught strategic management and international business programs. Jonas is an advisor, lecturer and consultant to a number of international companies. He has enabled them to look to the future more creatively and to develop dynamic and workable strategies, and organizational solutions. In his spare time he is an art collector and backs one of Sweden's funkiest galleries.

CONTENTS

Foreword

IT'S NOVEMBER 10, 1986. Snow and ice are slowly beginning to cover the kingdom of Sweden. Outside, in the cold, ordinary people leaving their offices fill the slushy streets. Meanwhile, inside the conference center, it is air-con cozy. Backstage, one of the best-known and most highly respected Swedish leaders of industry is preparing to give a speech to a large audience. As usual, he has prepared himself meticulously. Nothing must go wrong. It is critically important that the listeners understand his message – because his message is powerful, based on years and years of experience running one of the largest corporations in the country. In fact, he is in charge of one of the largest companies in the world. Not only that. He has seen the future. Indeed, some even say he is the future. Adjusting the knot on his tie, Mr President of Big Business Inc. walks on stage with the air of someone with something very important to say. He clears his throat and begins to preach:

"The vast majority of industry and the vast majority of society is not built upon what is known as entrepreneurship. Companies and society are stable, routine operations. They have limited room for fantasy, but a lot of room for competence. We will produce tomorrow what we produce today, hopefully of somewhat better quality and to a somewhat lower cost. We cannot afford rapid shifts in production and we cannot make changes just because someone comes up with a new idea. If we did that our industrial might and our infrastructure would soon collapse. We need a little creativity – not a lot."[1]

At the end of his speech Mr President sits down. There is silence around the conference center. Seconds later, seemingly endless warm applause fills the air. A satisfied smile spreads across his face. They got the message. All's well. Adjust your seats, sit back, relax and enjoy the ride.

Ten years later, Mr President goes to bed after a nice glass of vintage port and a relaxing game of bridge. As his head hits the pillow, he looks forward to nine hours of sound sleep and then, tomorrow, another satisfying day at the office. More of the same. Clean shirt and tie. As his eyes close, he feels someone shaking him. It is not the third Thursday of the month, so he knows it is not Mrs President. His eyes open. Beside him is a 20-year old IT-millionaire with a pierced tongue. The young man is accompanied by a Russian fashion entrepreneur, a female investment banker, a transsexual politician (with a vague resemblance to Mrs President), a physics professor in a rubber suit and a Buddhist Hollywood-star. Behind them stand a management guru wearing nothing but boxer shorts and a young Chinese woman who claims to be a global expert on thermodynamics (plus her cloned other self). They all want to know if he is ready to do Funky Business. Now!

Crash! Boom! Bang!

Welcome to the age of accidents. Welcome to the age of constant alarm bells where surprise is all and no one can predict what will happen tomorrow.

If you want a book about the future – look elsewhere. This is not a book about the future. This is a book about the funky world in which we are living right now. The future is already here.

This book is a case of self-therapy. We wrote it in order to figure out who we are, where we are, what is happening and why? Even though we both work as Assistant Professors at the Stockholm School of Economics, this book is not based on traditional academic research. It is the result of our personal – sometimes indiscriminate, sometimes indeterminate – pursuit of funk. That's not to say that our ideas are the result of a guessing-game. It is simply that 10 to 15 years of rigorous academic training combined with the irrepressible zeitgeist has led us down some non-traditional avenues, freeways and dead ends of research. During the last few years we have read everything from *Administrative Science Quarterly* to *Rolling*

Stone; visited boardrooms and bad, bad bars; talked to prime ministers and hell's angels; and discussed, debated, argued and analyzed among ourselves. Our aim has been to uncover some structure in an apparently disorganized world through the simple technique of asking questions; questions of others, ourselves, the ideas and experiences of others, and our own ideas and experiences.

Our project started out as a journey into unknown waters with three explorers. Professor Gunnar Hedlund, a rare and true renaissance man, was instrumental in the development of our early thinking. In addition to being a dear friend and mentor, Gunnar was as close to a live *Encyclopedia Britannica* with hyperlinks you will ever get. The weirdest and wildest of associations and ideas marked his exceptional mind. To Gunnar, architecture, chess, Beethoven's symphonies, soccer, religion, economics, art and psychology were all related. Gunnar sometimes lost us on his wild intellectual excursions – then, with much sadness, we lost him. He passed away on April 18, 1997. He may be gone, but he is not forgotten. As a tribute to

Gunnar, his thinking, and his legacy, part of the proceeds from this book will go to the Gunnar Hedlund Award, an annual prize awarded to the author of the best doctoral dissertation in the field of international business.

Ideas do not grow in a vacuum. They are shared and developed. They are borrowed and, sometimes, stolen. Over the years, our ideas have emerged from a profusion of sources and inspirations. In addition to Gunnar, we owe a great debt to many other people. For ten years, Professor Jan-Erik Vahlne shaped and refined the mindscape of Kjell. Our colleagues at the Institute of International Business have been a great source of inspiration over the years. The head of the Institute, Professor Örjan Sölvell, has always backed us in our efforts. In addition, Associate Professor Ingalill Holmberg, head of the Centre for Advanced Studies in Leadership, as well as Jonas' other colleagues, have been faithful supporters.

Our Swedish publisher Jan Lapidoth persuaded and cajoled us to take the necessary time out of our schedules to sit down and write this book. He has remained a driving force throughout the entire process. Without our agents at SpeakersNet, Britt-Marie Hesselbäck and Sara Gazelius, we would still be discussing the possibility of a book in Kjell's office. Thanks for always being there for us – no matter when we call. Katarina Lapidoth has given the book its excellent graphic form. Her patience and attention to detail deserves our profound gratitude. It has also been a true pleasure to collaborate with Ylva Blumenberg who makes slides for our gigs and who combines world-class standards, application and inspiration in one person. The business writer Stuart Crainer helped hone our literary style. What started as a professional relationship turned into real friendship which we hope will last beyond this book. For all his help, we are most grateful. It's been a true pleasure.

Warm thanks should also go out to the hundreds and hundreds of managers, artists, lawyers, doctors, personal friends, family members and many others with whom we have had so many interesting discussions during the last few years. Without your comments, questions, calls for clarification and sincere support, this book would never have seen the light of the day.

Tune in and turn up the volume. Don't adjust your seats.

Kjell A. Nordström
& Jonas Ridderstråle

1
FUNKY TIMES

"A working class hero is something to be"

JOHN LENNON

We have won. This is the age of capitalist triumph. We have conquered the world from Beijing to Baltimore; St Petersburg to Singapore. Western political leaders can barely conceal their smiles as they tour new stock exchanges in what were once outposts of Communist might. The eyes of businesspeople glaze over with self-congratulatory pride when they are introduced to Chinese entrepreneurs who have made fortunes overnight. Since the fall of the Berlin Wall, triumphalism has been in the air. Capitalism *über alles*.

There is one small problem. Karl Marx was right. We should all catch the first plane to Heathrow, get in a cab and request Highgate Cemetery. There, under an ivy-covered monument, lie the decaying remains of the author of the *Communist Manifesto*, the Communist theorist, Karl Marx. A steady stream of visitors comes to the cemetery to view the last resting-place of the great man. Elsewhere in the world, crowds flock to view the decaying remains of Marx's disciples. We, too, should pay homage.

We should pay homage to Ho Chi-Minh. He may be in a crystal coffin in Hanoi with a controlled environment of 60 percent humidity and 22 degrees centigrade, but he has the consolation that he was right. The same goes for Vladimir Illich Lenin. Every 18 months he has a bath and is lowered into a mixture of water, alcohol, glycerine and potassium acetate.[1] Two weeks later, his skin is as soft as a baby's bottom. Some 75 years after his death, Lenin's mausoleum is no more than a tourist attraction for capitalist comrades from the West. Yet, in spite of such indignities and ironies, Lenin was right. As was Chairman Mao Zedong. Mao is now marketed with free market abandon – for a mere 50,000 Hong Kong dollars you can buy a 24-carat gold statue of

Capitalism über alles

the great helmsman from the Sing Kwong Jewelry & Gold Co. Place your orders for Erich Honeker's tea sets and Enver Hoxha memorabilia now. They were all dirty Communist dictators, but they were also right.

They were right because they subscribed to the Marxist view that the workers should own the major assets of society, the critical means of production. We now do. And, perhaps, we did all along but we just didn't have the insight to realize it.

Workers control the principal means of production. The Revolution Part 1 is over. Workers – people in software houses in Frankfurt; shipyard workers in Stavanger; creatives in Chinese ad agencies; suits in offices in Sydney; factory workers in Los Angeles; derivative traders in Singapore – use their brains and, sometimes, their brawn to create new wealth. In a modern company 70 to 80 percent of what people do is now done by way of their intellects. The critical means of production is small, gray and weighs around 1.3 kilograms. It is the human brain.

The human brain is gloriously complex and intricate. It uses holographic organizing principles – the parts reflect the whole. Laboratory research even shows that you can take away nine-tenths of a brain and it will still work.[2] Try doing that to your car or video.

Our brain is capable of outperforming the most powerful computer on earth. Some of you may draw our attention to the chess battle between the IBM chess computer, Deep Blue, and the human Gary Kasparov. In February 1996, didn't the computer eventually beat the human grand master? It did, but the victory was possible because both players adhered to the rules, the given number of possible strategies. The trouble for corporate chess players is that future competitiveness will not be about following rules. It will be about breaking old rules and making new ones. Future success will be about challenging current wisdom and moving your pawn from A2 to E7 in one move.

It seems that John F. Kennedy was also right – even now when the computing power on planet Earth is estimated to be larger than our assembled brainpower – when he said that, "Man is still the most extraordinary computer of all." People can be creative, come up with new ideas, invent new rules and sense emotions; computers cannot – yet!

The critical means of production is small, gray and weighs around 1.3 kilograms. It is the human brain.

While the human brain is celebrated as the most wonderfully designed, incredibly intricate mechanism, the matter of who actually owns it is blissfully simple. It is not controlled by shareholders, investment funds, or any other body. George Soros may be able to destabilize currencies and markets, but he has no control over your brain. Governments can issue all the propaganda in the world, but your brain is your own. It is controlled, for better or worse, by the individual.

The battle of brains

Perfectly formed and individually owned, the human brain is overpowering the traditional means of production – raw material, hard labor and capital. Try to think of one major, successful contemporary business organization that is brawn-based.

Not a carmaker. Manufacturing cars competitively in the new millennium is concerned with utilizing technology to manage logistics; to design and manufacture great products; to provide service support; and to communicate internally as well as with networks of suppliers and consumers. Value no longer resides in the metal or the engine. Instead, value lies with the intangible elements. Some 70 percent of the value of a new car lie in the intangibles.[3] The result is that the brawniest car producer will be the bankrupt car producer. Car manufacturing is not about mindless, repetitive tasks carried out on a production line. Henry Ford is long dead and so are his methods. Ford once lamented, "How come when I want a pair of hands I get a human being as well." Now companies are more likely to ask – who needs hands?

Not General Electric. In 1998, more than two thirds of General Electric's revenues came from financial, information and product services.[4] In the not too distant future, it is possible that GE Capital, which finances everything from washing machines to jet engines, will make more money than all the rest of the company's businesses combined. Jack Welch, head of General Electric, has admitted that GE Capital could amount to 50 percent of the company – not in terms of employees, office buildings, and parking lots, but in terms of profits. The undisputed king of heavy industry has gone soft, because nowadays the really hard stuff is the soft stuff.[5]

Entire countries increasingly compete on the basis of knowledge. If you think back, all countries became rich through a combination of natural resources, labor and capital. Think forward and these factors are no longer relevant. In our age, you cannot earn money from natural resources alone. Even the Pope, John Paul II, agrees. In his 1991 centesimus writings, he concluded, "At one time the decisive factor of production was the land, and later capital ... Today the decisive factor is man himself, that is, his knowledge."[6] Business success is, as a result, a matter of herding flocks of brains.

It doesn't matter whether we are talking about Germany, Turkey, the United States or Belgium, primacy of knowledge is the only thing we are left to compete with. Natural resources, labor and capital, are rapidly diminishing in importance. That's why Bill Clinton and Tony Blair talk about a "cold knowledge war". They are determined to create conditions facilitating brain gain rather than brain drain. The Cold War of the post-war years was about brawn – as symbolized by lines of tanks rumbling past the Kremlin; the new cold war is more subtle (it comes in lower case for a start), but equally crucial – it is brains battling brains. The author Salman Rushdie even argues that the best way to overthrow Saddam Hussein is to flood Iraq with products and ideas – not bombs and missiles.

The third knowledge revolution

Knowledge is power is a neat aphorism. It has been used for decades in a loose and vague sort of way. We said it, and we may have said it repeatedly and loudly, but, however loud we shouted, there was the underlying belief that it really wasn't true – the reality was that force was power or, perhaps, power determined what was considered as knowledge. Now, knowledge really is power. We can shout it *and* believe it. Use all the force you want. Bludgeon down walls; threaten and cajole. It won't get you anywhere if you are dealing with someone who is smarter, quicker and hungrier. A nimble lightweight will always beat a ponderous heavyweight – except in the boxing ring.

Neanderthal man is long gone; now, we must bid farewell to Neanderthal behavior and thinking.

Knowledge is the new battlefield for countries, corporations and individuals.

Skeptics might say that the role of knowledge in money-making activities is nothing new. They would be right. In 1455, mankind saw the dawn of the first knowledge revolution. Johann Gutenberg's invention of the printing press made information more widely available than ever before. Some 500 years later we were hit by the second wave when radio and television began to dominate our lives. Fantastically, the early 1990s marked the beginning of the third wave. As *Time* magazine put it, instead of 500 TV channels, we now have millions of websites.[7]

The scale and speed of the third knowledge revolution is what makes it so different. It is calculated that some 90 percent of all scientists who have ever walked the face of the Earth are alive right now. When the US Army fought the Vietnam War, only 15 percent of the soldiers had a college degree. During Operation Desert Storm, approximately 99.3 percent of the soldiers were college graduates.[8]

Knowledge is the new battlefield for countries, corporations and individuals. We all increasingly face conditions that demand more knowledge for us to function and, in the long run, for us to survive. You can't build a wall around knowledge. You can't isolate it. It is there. It is crackling down phone lines. It is in the air, in cyberspace. It envelops the human race.

The rapid growth of the World Wide Web makes almost anything available to anyone, anywhere and anytime.[9] If knowledge is power, power now potentially resides everywhere. The scale of the changes, and of the opportunities, makes this a genuine revolution. In such times we are all condemned to being perpetually un(der)educated. Or as Socrates once said, "I know nothing except the fact of my own ignorance."

The revolutionary manifesto moves around the world with frightening speed. Once you could have a monopoly on knowledge, as an individual or a company, for a fairly long period of time. If a company had a smart idea in 1950, it took a while for others to jump on the bandwagon or even to find out. The archetypal firms of the early and mid-twentieth century were companies like the UK glassmaker Pilkington, the South African mining company De Beers and the American giant Xerox. These companies often had as long as 20 or even 30 years to globally exploit their firm-specific advantages – the stuff that made them unique.[10] They could use an incremental and sequential internationalization process, gradually adding nation after nation.[11] They conquered Argentina, then moved on to Peru and so on. The world could be inexorably dominated.

If knowledge is power, power now potentially resides everywhere.

This is no longer the case. Today, knowledge spreads internationally and instantly. Business best practices move faster than ever before. Business schools and universities spread the word with remorseless efficiency. In the 1960s, US business schools graduated some 5000 MBA students per year. Today, that figure is 75,000.[12] Back in 1967, two such MBA programs existed in the UK. In 1995, 130 programs were up and running.[13] In the US, there are now nearly 800.[14] Around 100,000 MBA graduates are let loose on the world every year. As they nurse their graduation hangover, they might like to contemplate the fact that much of their knowledge is already out of date.

Knowledge spreads. The Danish hearing-aid company Oticon launched a different way of organizing itself – project organization instead of regular hierarchy, no papers, new office architecture, etc. It was innovative and imaginative. Jack Welch of GE launched the concept of a boundaryless organization – transforming the whale into a shoal of dolphins. But before long, such bright ideas are written up in case studies. Organizations benchmark. They look around. The word spreads. Other companies copy Oticon and GE. Like some deadly virus, once knowledge is out there, it cannot be stopped.

Revolutions revisited

The fact that Karl Marx and his dictatorial disciples were right does not mean that we are reconstituted Communists. While they were right, they were far from being entirely right. Indeed, they may only have been right about one small thing. If you look around, the rich have never been wealthier. If you look around, capitalism has never looked healthier.

Of course, not everyone agrees with this view of the world. Complacency is easily found. In one of his execrable and lengthy sermons, the Cuban leader Fidel Castro informed his long-suffering people that they were going through *un periodo especial.* Castro promised that normal service (or lack of service if you are Cuban) would be resumed shortly. Castro advised his people to sit tight, wait and relax. They are probably still waiting. It is not often that you encounter someone who is totally, completely, absolutely, 100 percent wrong. But, Castro is. Revolutionary zeal has turned into wishful thinking.

Like it or not, change cannot be turned on and off. At the moment it is flowing uncontrollably. Put your hand over it and the water will spread in all directions. Sit back and you will drown. Welcome to the real revolution, Fidel.

The reality is that the revolution we are currently experiencing is bigger than even that imagined by Marx. It is a revolution that will change the very nature of our societies, economies, industries, firms, jobs, and personal lives. It is all-embracing. And it is happening now. You may not be able to see barricades in the street and tear gas filling the air, but it is happening – in all our minds.

In all likelihood you have never experienced a revolution. Nor have we. But, we know that during revolutions you throw out the rulebook. Revolutions are lawless, spontaneous and dangerous. We are not suggesting you begin looting, but, rather, pointing out that in this new environment, there are no rules, there are no laws, nothing is given. There is constant motion – perpetual crisis.

Traditional roles, jobs, skills, ways of doing things, insights, strategies, aspirations, fears and expectations no longer count.

In this environment we cannot have business as usual. We need business as *unusual*. We need different business. We need innovative business. We need unpredictable business. We need surprising business. We need funky business.

Funky business is truly global

No kidding this time. Internationalization has gone through a number of false dawns. Now it is the real thing. There are no borders for Luciano Pavarotti. Madonna knows no borders. Ford does not care about nation states. Terrorism cuts across the globe

tijd time	vlucht flight	naar to	uitgang gate	bijzonderheden remarks	
13:00	UL 564	COLOMBO PARIS	C39	DELAYED	14:30
13:10	DL 081	NEW YORK	C40	DELAYED	15:00
13:25	DL 039	ATLANTA	C42	NOATBOARDING	13:12
13:30	KL 621	ATLANTA	C47	NOATBOARDING	13:44
13:40	AF 1253	PARIS DE GAULLE	C43	NOATBOARDING	13:13
14:20	PK 721	NEW YORK	C46		
14:25	KL 833	DENPASAR SINGAPORE	C45		
14:30	TG 917	BANGKOK	C44	NOATBOARDING	13:48
14:30	ZA 107	CAIRO	C43		
14:45	SR 793	ZURICH	C42		
15:30	AT 967	CASABLANCA AL HOCEIMA	C38		
17:00	AF 1255	PARIS DE GAULLE	C38		
17:15	KL 329	PARIS DE GAULLE	C44		
17:30	AY 846	HELSINKI GOTHENBURG	C39		
17:35	KL 343	MILAN LINATE	C46		
18:05	KL 177	COPENHAGEN	C47		
18:40	AF 1261	PARIS DE GAULLE	C38		
19:20	KE 911	ROME FIUMICINO	C45		

We travel the world and the seven seas

– you never know where private terrorist Ossama bin Laden will strike next.

And, we have never seen a larger economic space. During the last 40 years, international trade has increased by 1500 percent.[15] No wonder, when average tariffs have simultaneously decreased from 50 percent to less than 5 percent.[16] We travel the world and the seven seas. We have global satellite channels, international magazines, TV shows, movies, hit records, etc. The global village envisaged by Marshall McLuhan in the 1960s is here.

Capitalism is on the move. Look at Eastern Europe and the former Soviet Union. There are more than 20 new nations – such as Belarus, Ukraine and Georgia. They are poor but want Western affluence as quickly as possible. So, they have been exporting madly. They export pulp and paper products. They export software. They export chemicals. In fact, they export everything they have. They are cold – freezing to death – and still export coal. They are the new competitors.

Many more are joining the throng. A few years ago, outside the OECD there were roughly 200 million people with realistic notions of joining the capitalist march. Countries like Japan, Singapore and Hong Kong were coming up fast. They were within reach. Now, 3000 million people are on the move. They come from the Indian subcontinent (900 million people), the former Soviet Union (220 million), Poland (55 million), Vietnam (70 million), Pakistan (130 million), Indonesia (160 million) and so on. They are all in the process of building lives and societies similar to those in the West. They would like the same comfort, material possessions and decadence. They will achieve their objectives. It is simply a question of when.

In India, 200 million people already have the same standard of living as the average European (in purchasing power parity terms).[17] At this moment, in Bangalore, 140,000 IT engineers are at work.[18] Bangalore is now the world's second largest city for software development. Novell is there. Siemens is there. Ericsson is there. In fact, more than 20 percent of the *Fortune 500* companies are there.[19]

Multinationals are not in India for charitable purposes. Think how much these Indian engineers earn. The answer is anything from $500 to $1000 a month.[20] Why would you hire anyone from Sweden, Germany, France, or the US, when Indian engineers work so cheaply and the quality of their work is identical to that found in our supposedly advanced societies? The economics could not be simpler; the ramifications could not be more profound. So tough is the competition from the experts of Bangalore and beyond that some of the most prestigious US universities – including Stanford, Berkeley, and UCLA – already operate a quota system to limit the number of non-US students. The stark truth is that, competing on grades alone, many US students would not stand a chance against their Asian fellows.

In the global village we can't do it alone. We need to find world-class partners. We need the best – the best architect, the best supplier, the best consultant – rather than the closest. This is already happening. The intermediary products that make up Ford's Escort model come from 15 countries. These include not only raw materials, but components and entire systems which come from a worldwide network of subcontractors and suppliers. The cars are finally assembled in two plants, one in the UK and one in Germany.[21]

Similarly, DRAMS – dynamic random access memories – are made in Southeast Asia, exported to Mexico for assembly as laptops and PCs and then shipped to markets throughout the world.[22] Such arrangements are now commonplace and, clearly, have enormous effects on companies and societies.

The economic realities of our time mean that everybody competes with everybody else. All of us are in global competition. Individuals are in global competition. Companies are in global competition. Countries are in global competition. There is nowhere to run and nowhere to hide. For us. For you. For Fiat. For U2. For Ricki Lake. For Robert De Niro. For Meg Ryan. For Augusto Pinochet.

Funky business means more competition for everything everywhere

In the West we have been brought up with the belief that more is good. This is not necessarily true. But, more is certainly evident wherever you look. More products; more markets; more people; more competition. More is a fact of life.

In 1996 at the Atlanta Olympics, Sweden won two gold medals. When the medallists returned to Stockholm, they held a press conference at the airport. One medal winner pointed out that athletes from 53 nations took the 271 gold medals on offer at Atlanta. Four years earlier in Barcelona, 37 countries won gold medals. She predicted that at the Sydney Olympics in 2000, 80 or 90 nations would be able to win a gold medal. If you are an athlete you don't know where the competition is going to come from next.

A similar rule applies elsewhere. Even the hallowed and sheltered halls of academia are not immune. We teach at the Stockholm School of Economics. There are some 5000 applicants

Stockholm School of Economics

every year for just 300 places. Those who succeed have the highest grades in every single subject. The School was founded at the beginning of the twentieth century to educate the élite of the élite. Twenty years ago if you were Swedish and interested in business administration and economics our school was the only real choice. The same was largely true just five years ago.

NEW YORK=WARSAW=STOCKHOLM=TEL AVIV =BERLIN=BANGALORE=COPENHAGEN

Now, bright, 20-year-old Scandinavians look around. They look at the Universität zu Köln, London Business School, SDA Bocconi in Italy, INSEAD in France and Duke University in North Carolina. They weigh up the pros and cons. They compare the schools. Stockholm used to be the only choice; now it is one of more than 1000. And things will only get worse – or better depending on who you are. The net will spread so that students automatically consider (so far unbuilt) Asian business schools or even schools in cyberspace. You can obtain a perfectly acceptable MBA if you stay in Lapland, buy a PC, read your Michael Porter assiduously and never leave home.

We are moving toward what academics call techno-economic parity. Techno-economic parity implies that that there are very few commodities, technologies, products, services, insights, knowledge areas or procedures in London, Paris, New York, Milan and Madrid that are not also available to our friends, brothers and sisters in Bangalore, Seoul, Gdansk, Buenos Aires and Kuala Lumpur. Techno-economic parity also implies that the basic prerequisites for doing business are becoming more even by the day. The playing field once had a slope as steep as Mont Blanc. Now it is being forced to the horizontal. In essence, techno-economic parity means that the best man or woman wins, no matter where they come from. The industrialized world no longer has a knowledge monopoly because knowledge moves freely. So we all need to prepare for the "Business Olympics". And, this event is not held every four years. It is happening now – in real time, non-stop.

Funky business requires a constant search for differentiation

In the wild market economy which now exists it is increasingly difficult to differentiate yourself. If you think about it, most of what your business does could be bought from someone else using the Yellow Pages or an Internet search engine. If you have a unique idea your competitors will steal it in two or three weeks. With three billion people in the process of building lives and societies similar to our own, competitive pressures are reaching boiling point. And they will keep on simmering.

There is only one way out. It is deceptively simple, do something else; do something that the world has not seen before. Innovate so that you are, for a moment in time, unique and uniquely competitive.

But, be warned, you will have to be unique in new ways. The old way of achieving uniqueness was to add a few extras to your product. This no longer works – it will be copied within days, perhaps hours, and consumers are no longer so easily fooled.

Organizations, services and products are becoming more and more similar. Often, you need a microscope to spot the differences. In the United States, the car industry waits expectantly for reports from the rating institute, J.D. Power. Its final report for 1996 began with the observation that, "There are no bad cars any longer, because they are all good." The car companies, whether they are Audi, Toyota, Ford or Renault, understand all the technology at their disposal. They understand each other's products. They take them apart and examine their innermost workings. Differentiation in the car industry must, therefore, come from other areas.

The new competitive battlefield is not the engine or the air conditioner – it is the design, the warranty, the service deal, the image and the finance package. Intelligence and intangibles. And, of course, people. People can make your organization, your products, and your service solutions unique. How you manage and lead people, how you organize your operations, will determine whether or not you succeed.

As a result, we need to rethink our definition of what is really valuable. According to *The Economist*, the new acid test is whether or not it hurts when you drop your competitive advantage on your toes. If it does, you should start rethinking the way in which you operate. Things that were in demand used to consist of a little knowledge and a lot of stuff. The new valuables are made up of a little stuff and a lot of knowledge.

Competitive advantages weigh no more than the dreams of a butterfly.

The average weight of a real dollar's worth of US exports has more than halved since 1970.[23] The density of a successful customer offering is changing. Today, competitive advantages weigh no more than the dreams of a butterfly.

Funky business requires organizational innovation

Organizing is the art of achieving extraordinary things with ordinary people. In our times, organizational innovation means creating conditions that enable a constant flow of creativity, not the churning out of yet another standardized product or service. Therefore, the funky firm needs to be different, look different, and work in new ways.

Percy Barnevik is the CEO of ABB, the Swiss/Swedish electrical engineering giant. His father, Einar, had a small print shop in Uddevalla on the west coast of Sweden. Percy grew up in this print shop. Often, he went there after school to help out his father and the other 12 employees.[24] Some 30 years later, he ran ABB, one of the largest companies in the world with approximately 220,000 employees worldwide. During his ten years as head of the company, Barnevik dedicated himself to trying to split ABB into some 5000 small units, with about 40–45 people in each unit. He wanted to re-create his father's print shop. Eventually, 1400 of the units were incorporated as companies in their own right. Barnevik says that he would have incorporated every single one of them as separate entities if it hadn't been for all the paperwork.

So why did Barnevik spend years tinkering with the company's organization? After all, it is an enormous amount of work. You have to redesign the reward system, redesign the budget system, redesign each and every little system of one of the

largest companies in the world. Barnevik's explanation was simple: there is not a single product, service, drawing or technology within ABB that Siemens or GE couldn't come up with within a couple of weeks. Whether it is Siemens, GE, Mitsubishi or ABB, the winner will be the company that is able to organize and manage its operations in the most innovative way.

All modern companies compete on knowledge, but knowledge is perishable. We must treat it like milk – we have to date it. Unless we use the knowledge of our firm, it becomes sour and loses its value. Continuous innovation, both revolutionary and evolutionary, is a necessity. Or, as David Vice, CEO at Northern Telecom, famously put it, "In the future there will be two kinds of companies – the quick and the dead."[25] We are either fast or forgotten. In the new economy, there are no speed limits. Agility rules. Speed is all. The need for renewal is something that applies to everything in the organization; it concerns everyone, goes on everywhere and is non-stop. "We intend to move as fast as we can, ripping up the road behind us," says Intel's Craig Barrett.[26] And he means it. Look around and the advice is simple:

No speed limits. Agility rules

Move it. In 1995, 1000 new soft drinks were launched on the Japanese market. A year later, 1 percent of them were still for sale.

Move it fast. If you are driving a 1990 model car, approximately six years were spent developing it. Today, most companies do that job in two years.

Move it faster. At Hewlett-Packard, the majority of revenues come from products that did not exist a year ago.[27]

Move it now. In Tokyo, you can order a customized Toyota on Monday and be driving it on Friday.[28]

Funky business puts management and leadership center stage

Leadership and management are more important than ever before. Gurus and commentators have been proclaiming this for years, maybe because it justified their existence. Now it is a reality.

This is the age of time and talent, where we are selling time and talent, exploiting time and talent, organizing time and talent, hiring time and talent, packaging time and talent. The most critical resource wears shoes and walks out the door around five o'clock every day. As a result, management and leadership are keys to competitive advantage. They differentiate you from the mass. How you attract, retain and motivate your people is more important than technology; how you treat your customers and suppliers, more important than technology. How a company is managed and how a company is led are vital differentiators. They can create sustainable uniqueness. But at the same time as management and leadership have reached maturity as potent competitive weapons, their very nature has changed.

The boss is dead. No longer can we believe in a leader who claims to know more about everything and who is always right. Management by numbers is history. Management by fear won't work. If management is people, management must become *humanagement*.

The job is dead. No longer can we believe in having a piece of paper saying job description at the top. The new realities call for far greater flexibility.[29] Throughout most of the twentieth century, managers averaged one job and one career. Now, we are talking about two careers and seven jobs. The days of the long-serving corporate man, safe and sound in the dusty recesses of the corporation, are long gone. Soon, the emphasis will be on getting a life instead of a career, and work will be viewed as a series of gigs or projects.

Inevitably, new roles demand new skills. Thirty years ago, we had to learn one new skill per year. Now, it is one new skill per day. Tomorrow, it may be one new skill per hour. Skills like networking – in 1960, the average manager had to learn 25 names throughout their entire career; today we must learn 25 new names every single month. Tomorrow, it may be 25 new names per week (and half of those are likely to be names from different languages).

Funky business gives us the power

No jobs but more power. We now own the major assets of society – our own minds. And power equals freedom. We are all potentially free to know, go, do and be whoever we want to be.[30] We can choose. We can be picky. It is up to us. But freedom is not something you are simply handed. It is something you conquer. And, today, power lies in controlling the scarcest of resources: human intelligence.

We are all potentially free to know, go, do and be whoever we want to be.

The more unique we are – the better we will do. And, as opposed to physical resources, knowledge grows with usage and is portable – you can take it with you when you leave. So, if you really want to build a good life – and/or just make money – the route to success couldn't be clearer: get at it and get going. The power is yours to use and abuse.

Into the funky future

With the introduction of the plantation we moved from the hunting and gathering society into the agricultural one and, with the coming of electricity, we entered the industrial era. Lenin once said that Communism equals electrification plus power to the Soviet people. Funkyism equals information mania plus the power of choice. Some call our world the knowledge society and others the brain-based one. The only certain thing is that the critical skills and answers of tomorrow will not be those of today. More important, however, may be the fact that the relevant questions are changing. Paradoxically, the ability to forget – unlearning – is becoming a key asset in a business world changing at the speed of light.

What is is

Change then change again. We are facing a world of chaos and genuine uncertainty. The new realities have been pithily described by GTE's Kent Foster as, "Products that are still evolving, delivered to a market that is still emerging, via a technology that is still changing on a daily basis."[31] It won't slow down for you to understand what is going on or to take a snapshot. In such a world, the only thing that we can trust is that the certain becomes uncertain, and the unlikely becomes likely.

The future cannot be predicted – it has to be created. Either you see things happen or you make them happen. You may be tempted to categorize the ideas and trends discussed in this book as good or bad, black or white. Resist temptation. Evolution is not right or wrong – it just is. We may use electricity to kill people or to make toast. Electricity is. The Internet can be used to distribute child pornography or to meet your future spouse. The Internet is. The future does not exist. It is not good or bad. It becomes what we make it. "What is is," says the Dalai Lama (while Bill Clinton labors over the exact meaning of is). Funky is.

Funky business means there will be many more questions with fewer and fewer universal answers. Einstein was wrong. No single theory can guide us. Diversity rules. Questions rather than answers fundamentally drive the future. And along the way do not expect much help from technology, because, as Pablo Picasso once pointed out: "Computers are useless. They can only give us answers."[32] But, if you ask smart questions, in a unique way, faster than anyone else, you will be momentarily ahead of the game. Enjoy it. Seconds later you have to think of the next question. Then the next.

2

FORCES OF FUNK

"I am the trouble starter
–punkin' instigator"

THE PRODIGY

If you are in danger of underestimating the new funky world, simply recite a selection of the facts below. Expect the unexpected. Forget fact-checkers, now we need funk-checkers.

In 1999, his holiness, Pope John Paul II, launched a CD *Abbà Pater* on which he raps. In a collaborative effort with techno and ambient musicians, the Pope goes pop.

 The terrorist group die Rote Armé Fraction sent a letter to the media declaring that it was closing down its operations. It claimed that there was no longer any fertile ground for its ideas.

God and Mammon finally join hands and make friends. A UK university now offers an MBA in church management.[1]

Article 11 of the Chinese constitution has been revised to read: "Private businesses [are] ... an important component of the country's socialist market economy."[2]

The GE factory in Louisville, Kentucky, was built in 1953 and has 25,000 parking spaces. Impressive. The problem is that in 1997 the factory only had 10,000 employees.[3]

Gucci's Kelly bag, which costs some 80,000 FF, takes 17 hours to produce – 2 hours more than the average car.[4]

Put up for sale by Fiat: its ski-resort in Sestriere; its 47 percent stake in the soccer club Juventus; its motorway business; and the port of Genova.

The world is a stage. We all play roles – organizations as well as individuals. But instead of conventional costume drama, we now have constant, unscripted, improvised theater. The director has left, the original play has been cancelled and the script is missing. The spectators are pouring on to the stage, joining the actors, demanding leading roles. Boundaries are blurring. Every role is vacant. Old rules no longer exist – the goodies and the baddies are the same person. Everything is up for grabs.

We are all contributors to the new society developing in front of our eyes. It is horrifying. It is fantastic. It is frightening. It is fun. It is depressing. It is weird. It is the funky village.

And if the world is being propelled headlong down a corridor of endless uncertainty and unceasing surprise, you would be justified in asking what forces are pushing us at the speed of sound? Who closed down the theater, sacked the director and shredded the script? What has got us into such a funk?

We do not believe there is anything particularly mysterious about the forces behind the revolution we are now witnessing. Revolutions are never subtle events. Tidiness and order aren't paramount as you storm the palace. At times of radical change, nuances are usually notable by their absence. We believe the three drivers moving us forward into the unknown are changes in technology, institutions and values. None operates in a vacuum. All overlap and interlink. Their impact is on each other as well as on society, companies and individuals.

Technology: the endless riff

Technology – in the form of biotechnology, information technology, transportation technology and many other guises – is reshaping our world. Technology is the rhythm section of funky business. Management guru Tom Peters provides a pithy summing up of where we now stand: "The nerds have won." Welcome to Nerdville.

Technology is not just a matter of nuts and bolts or bits and bytes. It is not a sideshow, but the ultimate in mass participation. It is curious – and a little daunting – to think back just a few decades. In the 1950s, 1960s and 1970s, technology was the domain of the military, rocket scientists, obscure academics and professors working in the R&D departments of pharmaceutical companies. Technology was Nobel laureates, Uri Gagarin, Apollo, missile systems and radar. Then it became commercialized, hijacked by entrepreneurial geeks. Creators of weapons of mass destruction dumbed down (or *dumbed up*, depending on your prejudices) to become instruments of mass entertainment.

Technology is the rhythm section of funky business.

Take the computer company SiliconGraphics. Ten years ago this company's most sophisticated customer was the US Army; now it is Mickey Mouse. When SiliconGraphics gets a new request from Walt Disney's Michael Eisner or Steven Spielberg, the engineers know that their paymaster is on the line. Today, it is movies and computer games rather than missile systems that frequently drive the most sophisticated developments in IT. Similarly, often it is retailers rather than manufacturers who lead the IT way. Software has the upper hand over hardware.

The riff of technology is unstoppable and irresistible. Axiom: technology is changing and will continue to change faster than any government can issue regulations to control it.

It is easy to forget how far we have come in such a short space of time. Alvin Toffler, a man with his eyes open to future possibilities, wrote his best-selling *The Third Wave* in 1980.[5] Look at it now and you will be startled. It was written so recently, yet the technological leaps made since its publication have been immense. Toffler, for example, has to explain what a word processor is – and mentions its alternative labels, "the smart typewriter" or "text editor". He envisages the office of the future: "The ultimate beauty of the electronic office lies not merely in the steps saved by a secretary in typing and correcting letters. The automated office can file them in the form of electronic bits on tape or disk. It can (or soon will) pass them through an electronic dictionary that will automatically correct their spelling errors. With the machines hooked up to one another and to the phone lines, the secretary can instantly transmit the letter to its recipient's printer or screen." In 1980 to the vast majority of Toffler's readers this read like science fiction. Now, it is reality to the vast majority of people in the industrialized world (or de-industrialized world, according to Toffler's perspective). To some, it is already dusty history.

Digital data

The central contribution of technology to funky business is in creating information systems. The impact of information technology is omnipresent. Today, information flows freely. You can't avoid it. It's like getting sand in your swimming trunks – a little annoying and close to impossible to get rid of.

The rhythm is never ending, like some mystical chant. Beat after beat. Today, there is far more computing power in the average car, than there was in the first Apollo spacecraft that took men to the moon.[6] There is more computing power in a greetings card singing *Happy Birthday* than existed on planet Earth back in 1950.[7] One CD-ROM contains 360,000 pages of text.[8] Not so long ago the fax was an important technological advance. Who now trumpets fax technology? Ditto the electric typewriter (with memory!) Ditto the floppy disk (soon) – Apple's iMac doesn't use floppies.

If we were to see the same development in the field of air travel as that we have witnessed in the IT industry during the last 25 years, a flight from New York to Scandinavia would not cost $500 or more and take some 8 hours. In fact, by 2024 it would take under one second and cost less than one cent.[9] The downside would be that the plane would be tiny and would crash once a week – trivial matters with such a price/performance ratio.

The beat goes on. The current wave of digitization is already affecting us all. IT development continues to make huge leaps. Most people in the West have a mobile phone. Our homes may soon be gadget-filled temples of virtual reality – just like Bill Gates' but smaller.

The momentum is unstoppable for a variety of reasons. Think, for example, of how little fun it would be if you were the only one with a mobile phone, the only person with access to e-mail or if you belonged to a network of one. Ludicrous perhaps but it does lead to a more significant insight. "Metcalfe's Law" states that the experienced utility of belonging to an electronic network increases exponentially with the number of users. Put simply, it is more than twice as fun if there are two instead of one.

And then there are three, then four and so on. Once these networks reach critical mass, they explode. It appears such fun to join that people just cannot resist. They spread as remorselessly as ivy. Mobile phones and the Internet demonstrate Metcalfe's Law in practice. It is notable that the dissenting voices about either of these technologies are now rarely, if ever, heard. The Luddite traditionalists who cast the Internet as Big Brother have been silenced – many, no doubt, have signed up and are cruising somewhere in cyberspace. Those who continue to be critical usually miss the point – "Put me in a room with a pad and a pencil and set me up against a hundred people with a hundred computers – I'll outcreate every goddamn sonofabitch in the room," says the writer Ray Bradbury, mistaking the creative opportunities offered by technology for creativity itself.[10]

The phenomenon of Metcalfe's Law explains why IT converts are so eager to tell their friends to get wired. The more people who join, the more your own cellular phone, Internet connection, or website is worth. Academics usually refer to this as network externalities or the law of increasing returns. Here, old rules no longer apply: value decreases rather than increases with scarcity. Translation: to those who have shall be given (even more). By winning initial advantages or market shares, over time you will benefit from additional

Our homes may soon be gadget-filled temples of virtual reality – just like Bill Gates' but smaller.

positive spin-offs. The more known or used your customer offering is, the more people will want to use it. As a consequence, sooner or later, someone is probably going to start giving away whatever it is you are now selling. Give it away to gain these initial advantages and eventually kill all the others.

Digital dreams

New technology increases both nativity and mortality. Eras come and go. Winners rise and fall. Every now and then, the fundamentals on which society is built erode and our constructions collapse. The old must make room for the new. When shipping became a potent force for the creation of competitive advantage, cities such as Venice and Lisbon flourished. Later, railroads turned these cities into tourist attractions while new junctions became more critical. Then came the automobile. Then the airplane. Just as Petra in the Middle East lost its position as a leading commercial center and is now mainly of archeological interest, digitization will exterminate some species and enable new ones.

IT decreases time and space. We live in a shrinking world. Cyberspace – once described by author William Gibson as a "consensual hallucination" – is the seventh continent. We no longer have a workplace; we have a workspace – and a lifespace. The new immigrants will be virtual ones, taking jobs from someone else without even showing their faces. Instead of moving people, we are beginning to move their thoughts and ideas. It is an entirely new ball game – with entirely new rules. And, most organizations do not adapt – they die.

IT enables total transparency. People with access to relevant information are beginning to challenge any type of authority. The stupid, loyal and humble customer, employee, and citizen is dead. Voters are challenging politicians; subordinates are challenging managers; students are challenging professors; patients are challenging doctors; kids are challenging parents; customers are challenging companies; and women are challenging men. Anyone whose claim to fame rests on an historical information advantage is challenged – challenged by individuals, organizations and regions with direct access to the same information. It is a power shift. Power now belongs to the people.

Challenge is in the air because the digital world removes the emperor's clothes. It makes Bill Clinton transparent, GE transparent, the UN transparent. And, you, too, are transparent.

People with access to relevant information are beginning to challenge any type of authority.

IT enables us to be anonymous – you can build your own personality, cafeteria style, on the Internet. You can be anyone. You can be man or woman, old or young, black or white. You decide. But, IT does not make us invisible. On the contrary. We all leave tracks. Every time you surf the Net, you leave tracks. Every time you use your credit card, you leave tracks. Every time you make a phone call, you leave tracks. These tracks can be used for multiple purposes. Information can be used to capture criminals or customers – pedophiles or bibliophiles. Whether we like it or not, we are all becoming self-segmenting individuals. Companies, organizations and authorities can find out who else makes similar tracks; people who follow similar trails – our binary and imaginary siblings in cyberspace – and so can we.

Total transparency also has a tendency to reveal and expose those not really adding any value.[11] IT will mean the death of the intermediary as we know them – instead we will get infomediaries: information brokers.[12] Infomediaries are people and firms who eliminate unnecessary actors in the value chain by simultaneously functioning as purchase agents for customers and sales departments for sellers. They may be entirely new actors or just existing firms that take on this role themselves. Three years ago, more than 20 percent of American air-travelers were already purchasing their tickets directly from airlines.[13] The percentage will inevitably rise. Why give your money to a travel agent? Why give your money to a wholesaler? Why give your money to a traditional record company? Why turn to retailers when there are e-tailers?

IT perfects markets. In the beginning there were markets. We traded. People exchanged goods for goods, and then goods for money. Price became the carrier of information. In the local bazaar, all the information was available at your fingertips. You could see, feel and smell the tomatoes, fish, jewelry, or whatever. But, as products got more complex and geographical distances increased, information became scarcer and feedback slower. Uncertainty exploded. Markets began to experience problems.

In response, we began to build hierarchies and formed them into organizations. We made stuff in-house rather than buying it from someone else. Markets and hierarchies basically fulfill the same function – they handle human exchange. In reality, companies are nothing more than private planned economies. Man rather than money coordinates them. They are ruled by plans not price. Long-term contracts dominate at the expense of constant negotiations. The advent of hierarchical organizations meant that uncertainty could be artificially reduced. It worked. The efficiency gains were sometimes enormous.

In an information desert, companies rule. But now we are re-entering an information jungle where information is again available at our fingertips. We are back in the bazaar – though this time it resides in cyberspace, the Net neighborhood.

Day by day, markets are becoming more efficient thanks to information technology. Markets are beginning to consume hierarchies – business firms and other organizations. Instead of making everything internally, companies have started buying more and more things from the external market. Instead of vertical integration – acquiring your suppliers and sometimes also your customers – the new trend is toward virtual integration.

Rather than one big, fat cat, there are now several mean, lean kittens working together in networks. Business-to-business e-commerce is currently five times bigger than consumer e-com-

Information at our fingertips.
Back in the bazaar

merce. Come 2003, Forester Research estimates that business-to-business e-commerce will have a turnover of some $1.3 trillion.[14] By virtually linking up with other star performers we can swap inventory for information. At Wal-Mart, the gigantic US retail chain, 97 percent of goods never pass through a warehouse.[15] The goods go directly from maker to shelf to you. The digital supply chain operates in real time. When you buy a woolen sweater from Benetton, the entire network feels it – all the way back to the sheep. A signal is sent from the cash register and, instantaneously, digital dominoes start falling. Soon, the entire network knows that it's time to produce a new sweater. All organizations are being forced to e-engineer their operations. They are turning their businesses into bazaars.

IT affects us all and affects everything. Your competitors are never more than a click away. Markets are consuming firms wherever you look. All organizations are now information-based whether they are schools, the Red Cross, unions, the French Foreign Legion, rock groups or business firms. We are all becoming wired. The only difference is that some are good at using IT, while others are bad. Already, there are great geographical differences – not that long ago in the US there were 63 PCs per 100 workers – in Japan only 17.[16]

A manager at a major construction company told us: "The Internet is the best thing that has happened to the construction industry since the invention of the crane." It enables a construction company to organize work in a totally new way. Indeed, as will be discussed later, IT enables and forces us all to reorganize and reconceptualize our operations. In just five years, the Internet has moved from being a solution looking for problems, to opening up the possibility of an entirely new business logic. As sellers we can reach a larger market – in 2003 there will be 510 million potential customers.[17] Not only that, distribution costs can be dramatically reduced by transferring bits rather than atoms. Just look at digital newspapers and computer games. As consumers, we can not only enjoy better prices and more convenience, but also a wider selection. If you were to print the cyberspace-based bookstore amazon.com's product catalog it would be the size of 14 New York City phone books. In addition to convenience and lower prices, we can enjoy better service – instant feedback and advice on which items others with similar tastes have bought.

We are in the process of moving from revolution to relevance. But, revolutions take time. Research carried out by Paul David at Stanford University shows that it took 20 years for factories to

Organizations with lousy infostructures will look like 65-year-olds competing in the Olympic marathon wearing high heels and evening gowns.

reap benefits from the introduction of the electronic motor.[18] As noted more than a century ago by economist Alfred Marshall, "The full importance of an epoch-making idea is often not perceived in the generation in which it is made. A new discovery is seldom fully effective for practical purposes till many minor improvements and subsidiary discoveries have gathered themselves around it."[19] Change will not happen overnight. But it will happen. When? Professor Michael Hawley at MIT's Media Lab claims that, "When computing becomes as basic as Jockey shorts, as sexy as lingerie, as absorbent as Pampers, the result will be big change."[20]

Still, one certainty is that "infostructure", the electronic nervous system of the company, will become more important than infrastructure. Organizations with lousy infostructures will look like 65-year-olds competing in the Olympic marathon wearing high heels and evening gowns.

Institutions: remaking the mausoleums

The second driving force of change comes from institutions. Institutions are contractual arrangements, sets of agreements that bind people together within political parties, marriage, companies, groupings. Institutions are the slumbering bedrock of our world. They are all the social structures that we humans create to promote stability and predictability. Institutions rest in large mausoleums as we busily go about our daily lives. They have a sense of timeless permanence. Untouched and apparently untouchable, they are there. And, because they are there, they matter.

Traditionally, the role of institutions has been to simplify. Strong and stable institutions subsume our freedom. This reduces uncertainty. We are free, but within tidy parameters erected by our institutions. Institutions act as stabilizers, touches of gray to tone down the bright colors.

But though they look inert on the outside, institutions are continually developing. Institutions are changing in front of our eyes. They may appear to be sleeping giants but the moment our backs are turned they shift in their sleep never to regain their previous posture.

Appearances can be deceptive. Confusingly, institutions often go out of their way to appear older than they actually are. Business schools, for instance, are institutions that like to give the impression of being older, and therefore more permanent, than they are in reality. A splash of ivy over the buildings is usually all it takes for them to convince themselves and everyone else they were there at the dawn of civilization.[21]

Institutions are not renowned for their creative, innovative or entrepreneurial abilities, but they are changing. They must. In a wired world, where knowledge can easily be detached from people and places, competitiveness will depend upon having the best systems and institutional environments. Success will depend on having a fertile ground for developing and utilizing knowledge; an environment in which ideas can be created, tried out, tinkered with, and exploited.

As new institutions develop, as there are what might be called institutional innovations, our lives are changed. The changes are not as obvious as when a bright new piece of technology impacts on our lives. Institutions do not – yet – come brashly branded in a box promising to halve our workload or weight.

But, think of the changes now happening within some of the major institutions that affect and influence our daily lives.

The institution of capitalism

At a macro level, institutional experiments abound. Communism, for example, was an institutional experiment that failed in the face of advancing technologies and changing values. Change did not come easily to societies built around five-year plans. Intellectual capital is difficult to explain and measure in a society in which capital is anathema.

After the fall of Communism, it would be easy to proclaim capitalism as the victor in the battle of institutional experiments. Celebration might be premature as there is now more than one type of capitalism. Indeed, there are *capitalisms*. These capitalisms are based, somewhat vaguely at times, on the same principles. But they are assuredly different. Even the most apparently fixed institution is built on shifting sand.

First, we have the European version of social-liberal capitalism with a fairly strong state that can and will interfere. (Do what you want up to a point.) Then there is North American market capitalism with minimal intervention. (Do what you want.) A third type is the Far Eastern collective capitalism built on trust and a very strong state. (We all know what we are doing and so does the government.) A final version is the robber capitalism or *cleptocracy* that we currently find in a number of the former USSR countries and in some parts of Latin American. (Do what I want or I'll shoot you.)

At this point, you may indeed look around and conclude that capitalism's rude good health is a figment of our imaginations. After all, we have seen a series of upheavals in major corporations with the downsizing demon wreaking havoc, as well as the Asian crisis and Russia's continuing problems in coming to terms with market forces.

We counter that capitalism is robust. It will carry on. But, the changes we are now seeing should not – and cannot – be underestimated. Capitalism is reinventing itself; carrying out a revolution from within. Revolutions are not over in a day or a night, they rumble on and on. It is like a movie with endless sequels. *Revolution* is followed by *Revolution II* then *Revolution III* ad infinitum. Unlike in the movie world, each has to outdo its predecessor. It is more like *Godfather* and *Godfather II*, one of the rare cases where the sequel actually outshone its predecessor, than *Rocky* and *Rocky II*.

The nation state

In *Triad Power* (1985) Kenichi Ohmae argued that countries are mere governmental creations.[22] In the emergent "Interlinked Economy" envisaged by Ohmae, consumers are not driven to purchase things through nationalistic sentiments – no matter what politicians suggest or say. "At the cash register, you don't care about country of origin or country of residence. You don't think about employment figures or trade deficits," Ohmae wrote. Ohmae is right. The nation state is no longer a relevant unit of analysis. The students who collect business school prospectuses from around the world aren't limited or even concerned about nation states. Tomorrow's high achievers don't care if they study in Sweden, Italy, Germany, Taiwan, Argentina, Iceland, Australia or South Africa. Their decision is made on the basis of what would be the best program for them. No more and no less. They look at the usual stereotypical things – where are the best looking girls and boys, the nicest beaches, the cheapest booze and the laziest classes? You may laugh, but remember that, with the

The nation state is no longer a relevant unit of analysis

exception of the last attribute, these may well be among the few factors that actually do provide the true sources of competitive advantage for a region in the future.

Multinational companies no longer think in terms of nation states. The furniture retailer IKEA will work with the best suppliers, wherever they may be. Why should you have a subsidiary in Finland, one in Norway and in Sweden? Obviously, you have a Nordic office. Why should you have a subsidiary in Austria and one in Germany? You have a subsidiary for the German-speaking part of Europe or whatever. Other units of analysis –

language, culture, age, climate, gender, lifestyle, sexual preferences, or whatever they may be – are more relevant.

The decline of the nation state is inextricably linked to the rise of internationalization as a potent force in business and beyond. In institutional terms, we are going through a period of globalization never before witnessed. For once, hype and reality are in accord. Whether it is through the European Union, the North American Free Trade Agreement or the Asian and Pacific Economic Cooperation, critical decisions are being transferred to a supranational level. We are building superstructures. Unfortunately there is not much evidence to suggest that superstructures are efficient. Maybe this explains why most modern business organizations are abandoning these solutions. The United Nations has long been a blunt instrument. The European Union is acting like an ambitious company of 20 or 30 years ago, wanting to do everything everywhere and, as a result, doing nothing very well.

From an economic perspective, the nation state is handing over the reins of power. We are living in a global economy. Today's markets are virtual and international rather than national. Information knows no boundaries. At a macro level, the critical problems and opportunities facing mankind can no longer be fruitfully defined as local ones. Unemployment is not a Dutch problem, nor a French problem; environmental pollution is not simply a German or a Turkish challenge. National efforts in such areas are commendable but they are, by their very nature, simply Band-Aids when radical surgery is required.

For such global issues, the nation state is far too small a unit for useful decision making. Unemployment, pollution, poverty and other such issues, demand larger bodies able to make bigger decisions.

Then paradox kicks in. At the same time as the nation state is too small a unit, it is also, in other circumstances, too big. Increasingly, the nation state seems unable – sometimes unwilling – to help us with our small problems. What about my children's school? What about healthcare for my grandmother? Can the nation state help me? The nation state appears caught in the middle: too small to make an impact on the big issues and too big to make an impact on the small issues.

Look at the Clinton Administration in America. On the big issues it had to make alliances with other nation states. Its victories were virtually all concerned with foreign policy and involved working in conjunction with other countries. When it came to the small issues that affect individuals it had a distinctly mixed record – the US healthcare system remains a shambles despite President Clinton's endeavors.

Political parties

Political parties used to be institutions built on ideals. Most modern parties, from left to right, started as single-question groups with the aim of changing the world. Over time they evolved into opinion conglomerates with views on healthcare, the school system, law enforcement, pension systems, military service, etc. The trouble is that people are no longer coherent in their views. It might be more useful if we all had ten votes to distribute between a number of parties, as they all have good *and* bad ideas. The attempts at unwieldy political coherence are out of step with our fragmented and incoherent perceptions and experiences of the world. As a result, the opinion conglomerates are losing legitimacy and gaining only contempt and disdain.

Not only that. Traditional political parties are also trapped in a geographical world. They are nationally structured. But, in global terms, who can make decisions that affect international capital markets, multinational firms and global superspecialists? Maybe, instead of hoping that the European Union or the United Nations can take care of all the global issues, and that any lack of global leadership should be handled by giving these institutions more power, we need to rethink our solutions more fundamentally. Perhaps, a more viable alternative is to establish a United Corporations. After all, the UN was set up at a time when the nation state was still a powerful and relevant unit of analysis. Today, companies rule the world, and this needs to be reflected in the institutions created to exert influence and control them. Even the ultimate benefactor of global supercapitalism gone wild, George Soros, echoes similar ideas.

The new political institutions are issue and problem-based, and they are global. They are organizations of the likes of Greenpeace and Amnesty International. The trouble for them comes when they seek to make the leap to mainstream acceptance – the Green Party in Germany has, for example, struggled to become a multi-issue party. Instead of being efficient external provocateurs, they find themselves having to adapt and ending up as toothless and impotent. As Sir Winston Churchill pointed out, "First we shape our structures – then our structures shape us."

The eternal enterprise

The bureaucratic firm is dead. It is just too small for effective exploitation and too big for energetic experimentation. As we shall see later (see Funky Inc.) the corporation is, and has to be, reshaped along entirely new lines. "Many companies need to reinvent themselves. And reinvention is not changing what is, but creating what isn't. A butterfly is not more of a caterpillar or a better or improved caterpillar; a butterfly is a different creature. Reinvention entails a series of continuous metamorphoses of this magnitude over time," says American consultant and academic Richard Pascale.[23]

At the heart of this reinvention is the realization that companies should not and need not be around forever. In the past, corporate success was measured, as much as anything, by the ability to survive.

There are many 80-year-old people who have had tedious, unproductive lives and many people who die young after lives packed with excitement and achievement. Much the same happens with companies. The prevailing view has been that permanence is good. This explains why companies build such vast headquarters buildings. The bigger the better; the deeper the foundations and the higher the tower, the better the business. In

Reinvent yourself

this world, the size of the company's atrium is important. Atrium-envy is the rule.

Longevity is attractive because it is better than dying. This is a tidy, but not very persuasive argument. Yet, faith is still placed in companies lasting a long time. If they are around for a while, surely they must do some good. Arie de Geus in *The Living Company* quotes a Dutch survey of corporate life expectancy in Japan and Europe which came up with 12.5 years as the average life expectancy of all firms.[24] "The average life expectancy of a multinational corporation – *Fortune 500* or its equivalent – is between 40 and 50 years," says de Geus, noting that one-third of 1970's *Fortune 500* companies had disappeared by 1983. Such mortality is attributed by de Geus to the focus of managers on profits and the bottom line rather than the human community which makes up their organization. Fix this, and you have discovered the fountain of youth.

But what if de Geus is absolutely wrong in suggesting that firms should aspire to live forever? Greatness is fleeting and, for corporations, it will become ever more fleeting. The ultimate aim of a business organization, an artist, an athlete or a stockbroker may be to explode in a dramatic frenzy of value creation during a short space of time rather than to live forever. Somewhat surprisingly, the places with the highest growth rates and most dramatic success stories, such as Silicon Valley and the Houston IT-cluster, also have an extremely high rate of corporate mortality.

For firms, this implies that the company becomes more disposable – a temporary camp for nomadic individuals who then move on to meet new people and challenges. After all, we have a disposable mindset in virtually every other area of life. Maybe we should, in the words of Sir Paul McCartney "Live and let die".

The disposable company is not a new phenomenon. Among the first enterprises we know of are the ancient vessels that sailed from upper to lower Egypt to collect gold, diamonds, and slaves. People invested in such ships and if and when they returned, the investors and the crew struck gold. After the journey, this specific enterprise was terminated. History repeats itself. So, don't be surprised if in the future it proves much more rewarding to be a reincarnating insect than a 300-year-old tortoise. The firm with a future, short-lived or not, is energetic rather than eternal. Listen to Canadian rock legend Neil Young, "It's better to burn out than to fade away."

Fading ideals?

The family

There is a mystical aura around the concept of family, a rosy glow of well-being. The family is the maternal bosom. It is the sugary sentimentality of *The Waltons*. It is mother and father standing proudly with their children. It is well-balanced and sophisticated; warm and uncomplicated; unsullied by reality.

Of course domestic reality is quite different from the saccharined sentiments served up by the advertising and media industries. No matter how bright, happy and sophisticated their members may be, families are all dysfunctional. It is simply a question of how dysfunctional.

There is little doubt that traditional notions of what constitutes a family are breaking down. Divorce rates are skyrocketing and a lot of young people never marry – they stay single or just live together. As it stands, the family could soon become a luxury item – happily married couples with 2.4 happy children (a pet dog, and a whitewashed house with a picket fence) will be

During the 1960s, US fathers on average talked some 45 minutes per day with their kids. Today, the equivalent figure is six minutes.

the exceptions, unusual archetypes of a fading ideal. Although laws and regulations do not always reflect it, for many the *de facto* standard is already, serial monogamy, threesomes, etc. Lots of kids are brought up without being exposed to long-lasting, permanent relationships. They may have two fathers and three mothers. Two of their brothers have another dad, and their sisters have a totally different set of parents. And then we expect them to work for one company and one boss for the rest of their lives!

And if people indeed do form families, they no longer spend that much time together. During the 1960s, US fathers on average talked some 45 minutes per day with their kids. Today, the equivalent figure is six minutes.[25] When the Norwegian furniture company Stokke launched its Tripp Trapp children's chair in France there was a disappointing response. Then it discovered why. Families did not sit down for meals together any more. Even in France, home of gastronomy and convivial meals, families eat at different times. There simply wasn't a need for a chair that allowed children to sit comfortably at the same height as adults. So, a Norwegian company had to set about re-educating the French to eat meals with their kids.

We are brought up with a set of notions. Previous generations called them standards and are fond of telling younger generations that standards have fallen. The reality is that standards have changed. Yet, when it comes to families we are still measured against previous family values. We consider ourselves to be failures. There is a nagging suspicion that we are aiming unreasonably high. Perhaps there is nothing wrong. We are just different.

When Stokke launched its Tripp Trapp children's chair in France it discovered that families did not sit down for meals together any more

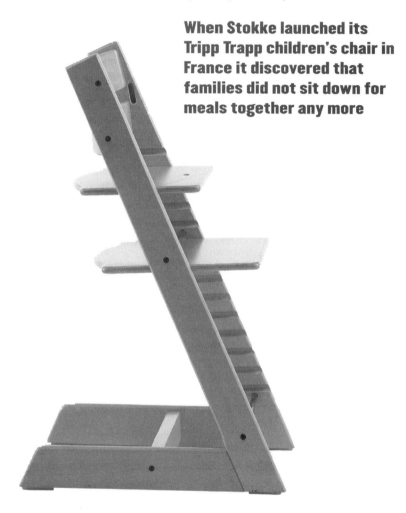

Values: from telescopes to kaleidoscopes

The final part of the triad of driving forces is value systems. For better or worse, values affect all of our thoughts and deeds. Values are the way we relate to work, technologies, and people. Values influence artefacts and actions. Values are enormously powerful, omnipresent and hugely different from place to place, person to person. Values create unity and conflicts. But values also change – slowly, very slowly.

Working values

Capitalism and Christianity are close relations. We would never have seen capitalism as we know it without the Protestant revolution resulting in a new work ethic. Martin Luther said that we should pray and work – *ora et labora* in Latin. Work in itself was good, an act of homage, spirit-enhancing and humbling.

The corollary of this is that the actual nature of the work is not that important. Work is good. And, if you spend 12 hours working on a machine carrying out repetitive tasks, work is still good. The act of work is good, therefore, you want to and need to work. Luther's edict produced generation upon generation of self-motivated workers. They wanted to work because work was the route to betterment.

Look elsewhere and value systems are at odds with basic Western conceptions. While work was the fulcrum of the Western world – and the basis of our initial industrial pre-eminence – the East embraced its own Luther: Confucius. Luther venerated work; Confucius venerated wisdom. In the Far East, many people start to save money for their children's education before they have even found a partner. In the East wisdom is all.

In Eastern economies many people believe in both Buddha and Confucius. Buddhism stands for horizontal solidarity and Confucianism propagates vertical subordination. What for most Westerners is a classical oxymoron and paradox – being simultaneously horizontal and vertical – is for these people the most natural thing in the world. Add capitalism to create a little direction, and you get a mean machine moving at the speed of light. Put Communism on top of this system, and you get another type of mean machine – there are far too many who can verify that particular fact.

Values differ. The Chinese economy is built on the concept of trust – *Guanxi* – a strong and inexpensive substitute for contracts and lawyers. This concept extends to the overseas Chinese who tend to cooperate wherever they are. They have created a global network in which knowledge and capital, goods and services flow freely. How much business would you do in the absence of contracts? If it came down to trust, how many colleagues, suppliers and customers would you really get involved with?

Values differ. In Japan, robots are named after famous singers. How many of you have an ABB Madonna at your job? A Japanese union's idea of a strike is a one-hour work stoppage timed for the lunch break.[26] As the firm is the family, the goals of employee and employer overlap. A strike during working hours would, therefore, be counter-productive – you would effectively be striking against yourself.

Values differ. Consider the case of Christmas. A few years ago, before the glorious arrival of Tamagotchi, Teletubbies and the Furby, one of us visited the Danish toy manufacturer Lego. Needless to say, Lego is interested in what kids want for Christmas – and it undertakes extensive market research to find out about their wishes. To the left are the results from the UK study of what 5 to 12-year-old kids want for Christmas.

The UK

Bicycle
Clothes (general)
Books
Clothes (sports)
Games (computerized)
Watch/clock
Lego
Computer
Sports equipment
Nintendo

With a few exceptions, British kids appear to want the same things that we wanted when we were young.

Meanwhile, Lego has a small market share in Japan but, as Japan is a potentially large and growing market, it wanted to find out more about the wishes of Japanese children aged 5–12. Here to the right are the results.

Who do you think will develop the customer offerings of the future – companies located in the UK or Japan?

Japan
Electronic diary
Cordless phone
Word processor
Personal phone
CD / radio / cassette player
PC
Fax
Telescope
CD mini-stereo
Keyboard

Fusion in the global village

Now, values have been geographically liberated. Value systems were once local. In our part of the world, the church was in the middle of the village and had a monopoly over local values. Now, next door to the church you are liable to find a mosque. We are continually exposed to different values. Assumptions have been replaced by a need for decisions. We have to choose. Do we visit the church or the mosque? What is the difference between the values of the two?

Often the end result is not as clear cut as it once was. Now we might believe in God while embracing other cultures and other values. The actor, Richard Gere proclaims his Buddhist beliefs while at the same time carrying on a successful career in the distinctly non-Buddhist surroundings of Los Angeles. We are internally consistent but, to the institutions and values outside, a bewildering juxtaposition.

The new reality is reflected in the make-up of management teams, football teams, what we buy, what we eat – Thai chicken wings (Buffalo-style) with pasta – how we live and who we are. Cultures, tastes, experiences, collide to create a cornucopia of values. Mongrel mania.

Fusion is too easily identified with confusion. The two do not necessarily follow. Japanese philosophies can operate successfully with Western philosophies. American companies can succeed in

Japan. But success will only come to those who appreciate and are sensitive to different value systems. Competition is now global and value-based.

As values have been re-combined in powerful fusions and moved beyond national boundaries, old assumptions have been tossed aside. There are no easy and generally held answers to questions about the value of material possessions versus knowledge, about right and wrong, good and evil. The questions remain, but the answers have become more blurred. For the first time in history, people from various parts of the world with partly different definitions of what constitutes what Socrates once called a "good life" are going to compete. Individualists against collectivists. Uncertainty reducers against uncertainty producers. All against all.

Spiritual emptiness

Behind all these effects we see a gigantic spiritual vacuum. It is a mist sweeping over the world filling us with doubts and hesitation. We are no longer pilgrims with a clear mission living in a well-structured environment. Instead, we have become wandering vagabonds in search of ...?

This trend is especially noticeable in a country such as Sweden. Its Welfare State and social systems were supposed to be the best in the world, and yet country after country now appears to be passing Sweden by. Perhaps it is time to start questioning the basic beliefs and to determine what values are still viable in a borderless information society.

Is this the end of religion? Do the Ten Commandments belong to the group of endangered species. How many of your friends regularly go to church and really believe in something other than themselves? French author Emile Zola was right back in 1886 when he observed: "We have stopped believing in God, but not in our own immortality." Is this the end of ideologies? No wonder that only half of the voters exercised their right to elect the new president of the US, "the world's greatest democracy", in

1996. In the 1999 election to the European Parliament, in many nations, less than 40 percent of the citizens voted. Democracy turns demo*crazy*. When people are only loyal to themselves, or whatever may be the worthy cause of the month, can we talk about the end of solidarity? We live in a world in which we buy letters of indulgence by watching Live Aid or sending a few bucks to Greenpeace.

Is this the end of the modern project? Have we given up the idea of building a society in which all people can prosper? Hasn't the acceptance of leaving a few lost souls out in the gutter risen during the last few years? And without soul, objectives, and meaning, is this not the end of progress? After all, if you have no idea of where you want to end up, it does not really matter which road you take?

Pope Paul VI foresaw this development some 30 years ago. He rightly claimed that, "Technological society has succeeded in multiplying the opportunities for pleasure, but it has great difficulty in generating joy."[27] So, welcome to a world of violence, sex, drugs and rock 'n' roll. A global freak show. Jerry Springerville.

Here is a list of the Products of the Year in 1994, identified by *Fortune* magazine. It is a few years old – Springerville is not a new discovery – but we still find it amazing.

Wonderbra
Mighty Morphin Power Rangers
Oldsmobile Aurora
RCA DSS
Baby think it over
Snake light
Mosaic
Svelte
Myst
The Lion King

Not much spirituality there: a bra sold with the slogan "bye-bye toes"; a plastic baby stuffed with electronics that teenagers can rent for the weekend to check out what parenthood is like; a lotion that reduces cellulite; and small plastic figures that fight evil warlords from outer space. An anorexic, big-breasted, electronic warrior is the ultimate product of our times.

Deregulating life: condemned to freedom

The three drivers of technology, institutions and values have created an international, knowledge-based world. In this new environment competition is total and personal. If knowledge is key we are all competing against each other. The genie is out of the bottle and cannot be put back in. People who spend their time trying to do so should not be approached, let alone employed. There is no going back. While a great many people recognize that the genie is out, few have sufficient insight to turn this recognition into action.

Freedom has been thrust back into our hands. Institutions used to work to create certainty. Now, the certainties are withering. Blind loyalty has died. We no longer proclaim lifelong loyalty to institutions, no matter what they are or what they do. We shop around. Lifelong membership is defunct, whether it be of a political party, a relationship, a fan club, a company or a country. We are more promiscuous about our institutions. Promiscuity is based on choice. Technology used to be concerned with mechanization. Now, it creates complex systems. Values used to be built around strictures and clear expectations. Now, values are a moveable feast as our value systems are liberalized.

We are deregulating the banking industry, the telecoms industry, the airline industry, etc. We are deregulating morally. We are deregulating technologically. As individuals, we could cross any boundary. Indeed, we are deregulating life for ourselves and for our children. They

Indeed, we are deregulating life for ourselves and for our children.

can freely choose where to live, what to do, where to work, what to study and who to be. They can choose to be homosexual, heterosexual, sadomasochistic or transvestites. They can choose when to work and when they want children, if they want children at all. We have the power of choice. It is the American dream to the max – total freedom.

Enjoy it. Tomorrow we are going to wake up in a world in which we all need to realize that we are condemned to freedom – the freedom to choose. There is no escape. Institutions won't shoulder responsibility because they are in a state of confused flux. There is no church, no nation state, no market to rely on. There are no cut and dried values to use as escape tools. Technology exists to create opportunities, to create efficiency, not to take responsibility from us. So, at the beginning of a new millennium, we are faced with the prospect of taking charge of our own freedom.

With choice comes responsibility. Responsibility for our own health, for our own education, for our own careers – responsibility for our own lives. The more opportunities there are, the more responsibilities there are for us as individuals. We have been given greater responsibility at a time when the old certainties have evaporated. The institutions, values and technologies that previously existed are disappearing. The decisions and choices of today and the future will be made in a climate of all-embracing uncertainty.

Coping with chaos

Chaotic times are here again. The trouble is that the human race does not react very well to uncertainty. Change inevitably leads to unrest. One generic response to this is to reduce freedom dramatically. The Fascist movements of the twentieth century emerged from periods of economic turmoil and uncertainty. People cried out for strong leaders – leaders who could reduce uncertainty. Today, the uncertain are as likely to join a religious sect as a political party. People join because the complexity and uncertainty of everyday life can be removed. They don't have to worry about income tax, office politics or their credit cards. They surrender doubt with certainty. True believers have, it is often said, a far away look in their eyes. For true believers this is literally true. They have opted out. The downside is that you always have to opt in to something – and if that something eliminates uncertainty and doubt, it is probably not good for your long-term mental health.

While a minority cope with uncertainty by disappearing into the distance muttering mantras and following their leader, others switch on the TV. TV convinces you that things could be worse. This, sadly, explains the rise of freak show TV as exemplified by the *Jerry Springer Show*. The show succeeds because it makes viewers feel normal. We watch TV to figure out ourselves, to be reassured that we're better off, mentally, physically or financially, than the freaks on display.

Avoiding uncertainty is human nature. Companies bring in consultants to buy uncertainty reduction. We can't figure out what is happening, so let's bring in some people who are really bright and have a model to deal with this sort of thing. The consultant's report is nothing more than a corporate comforter.

Throughout the business world there is a profusion of models, frameworks and assumptions. All are managerial versions of

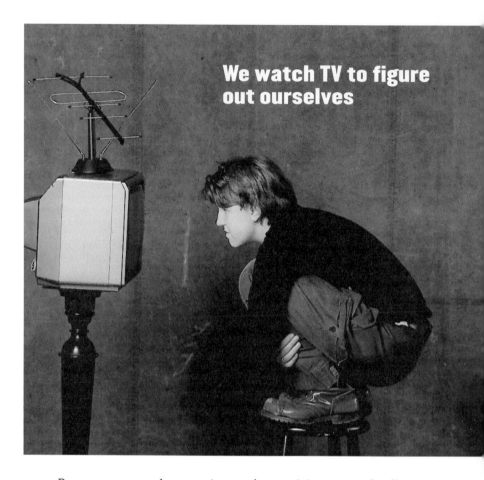

We watch TV to figure out ourselves

Prozac: guaranteed uncertainty reducers. Managers – hardly a breed associated with revolution – have created their own messiahs and their own religious sects in management gurus.

Uncertainty reduction is a ritualistic part of corporate life. When you start a job, you spend a day or two in an induction program. The organization tells you how to behave. It is dressed up in nice, friendly corporate language, but that is basically what is happening. We believe that such complacent corporate certainty now has to give way to complexity. We believe that the optimum response must be to embrace complexity – not try to eliminate it. Complexity is horrific but fascinating. We have to have the courage to face it.

It may save our sanity. After all, if you measure yourself against uncertainty, life tends to look a little better. In contrast, measuring yourself against certainty is irrelevant and depressing. If everything is in a state of flux the only fixed thing is the individual. A defined picture of yourself is as much as you can hope for.

In the recent past our roles were pre-defined. The Church or the corporation provided the historical script. No more. To be successful in a world of improvisational theater, you have to ask yourself questions. You have to know yourself and your objectives. It is Management By Objectives for individuals. Defining yourself is the only means of creating a good life. This gives leaders, anywhere in organizations, a new job. They must produce uncertainty. Real leaders challenge people. They do not control them. True leaders set people free.

面 埼京線 **3**
ya **Saikyō Line**

"The more the merrier"
PROVERB

We are so small and there is so much of everything. Look up at the stars and count. Look down from a plane and contemplate the lights. We are insignificant, overwhelmed by the seas of choice and the tides of change. There is so much. The trouble is we keep asking for more.

This is the age of more. More choice. More consumption. More fun. More fear. More uncertainty. More competition. More opportunities. We have entered a world of excess: an age of abundance. No wonder that Andy Grove of Intel claims that, "Only the paranoid survive."

It is a shock. Think back to the pictures you would see on the TV news in the 1970s and 1980s of Moscow's premier department store, GUM. The shelves were always completely empty. A rotund Russian stood at a bare counter. Behind him there was always a single bottle of extra-strength diesel fuel masquerading as vodka. The lonely Muscovite housewife lingered by the empty shelves dreaming of excess in a world of constraint.

We have entered a world of excess: an age of abundance.

That was then. This is now: think Saks Fifth Avenue, Printemps, Selfridges, amazon.com, Macy's, Galeries Lafayette, Harrods or Yahoo. Even in Moscow, bare shelves have been replaced by glorious excess. For bread and circus read champagne and caviar, canapés and trinkets.

Consumers of the world – congratulations! We were recently told that the Mall of America in Minneapolis attracts 40 million visitors a year – more people than Disney World, Disneyland and the Grand Canyon combined. Shop till you drop.

The surplus society

In Norway – population 4.5 million – you can choose from 200 different newspapers, 100 weekly magazines, and some 20 TV channels.[1] In Sweden – population 9 million – the number of beers to choose from has increased from around 50 to over 350 in little more than 10 years. The year of 1996 saw the publication of 1778 business books in the American market.[2] Major label record companies launched 30,000 albums in the US in 1998.[3] In the same country, the number of grocery product launches increased from 2700 in 1981 to some 20,000 in 1996.[4] To keep up with all the product launches, Procter & Gamble has more scientists on its payroll than Harvard, Berkeley and MIT combined.

Profusion abounds. The lady in GUM now has 47 TV channels and a quarter of a billion home pages to choose from

More of the same

(though the supermarket remains devoid of anything she can afford). Viva choice! Seiko turns out more than 5000 separate watch models.[5] In 1996, Sony launched 5000 new products – more than 2 new products per working hour. Maybe this is necessary in a market where the average product lifecycle for consumer electronics products is now three months.[6] Still, compared to Walt Disney, Sony's innovation record is nowhere.

Disney's CEO Michael Eisner claimed that the company develops a new product – a film, a comic book, a CD or whatever – every five minutes.[7]

Excess is in and the route to this world of excess is the TV. The temple of our times is not the Church, but the TV. The battle for our souls is acted out every weekday night as David Letterman, king of American late-night TV, fights it out with Jay Leno to capture the interest of the average John and Jane Does of the US TV audience. The concept is simple: ten minutes of talk followed by a commercial; then more talk and a commercial; more talk, more commercials. At the end of the day, the average American citizen has been exposed to some 247 ads.[8] By the time they reach the age of 18, they have encountered 350,000 TV commercials. And just wait until we get the Internet live on TV, fully interactive TV. It is coming soon to your living room.

Also knowledge is exploding. Think of the 140,000 IT engineers developing software in Bangalore. Think of the profusion of MBA graduates. Think of the leap in numbers of people going through college. Think of the flood of scientists. Think of the well-educated Desert Storm soldiers.

The world is alive with knowledge, with products and services, with information. But more often simply means more of the same. The surplus society has a surplus of similar companies, employing similar people, with similar educational backgrounds, working in similar jobs, coming up with similar ideas, producing similar things, with similar prices, warranties, and qualities. And even though they may not yet know it, all these firms, individuals and customer offerings are competing. This is good news if you are a customer; and time for prayer if you are an executive.

Three key forces lie behind the emergence of the surplus society: the growth in markets resulting in market mania; senseless oversupply; and technological advances which have made communication more or less costless. And behind these forces, we can again discern the influence of changes in technology, institutions and values.

Market mania

The first element in creating this world of excess is the growth in markets. There are now more markets for more things, covering a larger geographical area than ever before. Deregulation and trade liberalization have unleashed market forces on virtually every human activity. At the turn of the twentieth century, some 10–15 percent of the world population lived within a market system. In the 1970s, approximately 40 percent of all individuals lived within such a system. Today, we are talking about 90 percent.[9]

But not all markets are global yet. Take labor markets. Only 1.5 percent of the workforce works outside its home country. In the European Union, the equivalent number is 2 percent.[10] Capital still flows more freely than people.

Still, in this crazy world there are markets for absolutely everything. Markets in commodities and capital; body parts; every conceivable type of sex; any industrial component you can think of; and any kind of service you can imagine. There are markets in betting – spread betting applies the logic of the futures exchange to sporting bets; markets in alcohol – a Dutch nightclub entrepreneur operates a futures market in drinks at his clubs; and markets in knowledge and talent.

Feel the funk. If you want to – and can afford to – you can even hire Versailles to throw the ultimate office party. Some 200 years after the French Revolution, the Hall of Battles is yours for a mere $70,000.[11] Or why not choose somewhere a bit further afield, a little different – like the American investment bank which partied in the Forbidden City in the People's Republic of China. Everything has a price. Markets rule.

Senseless supply

In the recent past the world was a big place. Cutting-edge technological knowledge was to be found in the industrialized Western world. That was where the renowned universities, aggressive companies, and other competence-producing organizations, were based. This was the age before the joint venture and the strategic alliance; before collaboration was made easy through technology; before the explosion of new, different technologies.

In this world, demand mostly exceeded supply. After World War II, there was a great surge for new jobs, products and services. The European and Asian industrial infrastructures were in ruins. This was great news for any company in any industry. We were at their mercy – as employees and consumers. Moreover, the rate of technological change and proliferation of customer preferences was not as great as it now is. Things moved slowly and usually moved locally. This was the world of mass production where markets were assumed and taken for granted; where customers were told what they wanted – any color so long as it was black. Weighed down with managerial layers and with no apparent need to broaden perspectives, companies sailed on like supertankers on autopilot.

"In the slow-growth 1990s, overcapacity is the norm in most businesses."

The rocks are here and the lighthouse has closed down. In industry after industry, and in market after market, supply is beginning to exceed demand. Business professors Sumantra Ghoshal and Christopher Bartlett have noted: "In the slow-growth 1990s, however, overcapacity is the norm in most businesses: 40 percent in automobiles, 100 percent in bulk chemicals, 50 percent in steel, and 140 percent in computers, for example. Both technological progress and customer needs are driving toward smaller lot sizes and higher variety."[12]

Old local companies can, and do, now compete all over the world. New companies can, and do, now enter traditional industries. As firms no longer need to make everything that they plan to sell – they can buy it from someone else – entry barriers are evaporating. Totally new entrants, or firms that historically competed in other industries, can combine components from other companies. They don't need huge amounts of capital or specialist knowledge. Invisible invaders can attack conventional companies from all directions. Supply is surging – and it will keep on surging.

Costless communication

Finally comes the phenomenon of decreased communication costs. Information costs have dramatically plummeted. In 1930, a three-minute call from New York to London cost some $250 (in 1990 dollars). Thirty years later, the cost for a similar phone call was down to $50. Now, we are approaching zero.[13] Similarly, the cost of sending a 40-page document from LA to Washington is $9 by fax; $16 by FedEx; $3 by snail-mail; and 9 cents by e-mail.[14] The Internet provides zero-variable transaction costs – costs that occur when you do business (setting up and controlling contracts, etc.). Little wonder that Michael Dell has said that the Internet is only surpassed by telepathy.

Sending information has never been cheaper. Ditto searching for information. IT enables us to scan the entire market. We can scan the world. Armed with our search engines, we are no longer restricted to the special offers in our neighborhood. CompareNet, for instance, offers detailed information on more than 100,000 consumer products.[15] The flood of information allows us to always find the best deal. Infomediaries are already a powerful force. Some 16 percent of all US car buyers shop on-line before turning up at a dealer.[16] The Internet, or any other source of processed information, makes comparison shopping a picnic.

The return of the demanding customer

We are moving toward increasingly perfected markets. The result is total competition. In the surplus society the customer is more than a king: the customer is the mother of all dictators. And this time it's for real. If the customer speaks you have to jump high and jump fast. The customer wants products in orange with purple spots. The customer wants them today in Fiji. You have to deliver otherwise you will soon be out of business. As Lou Gerstner, Chairman and CEO of IBM, put it at the OECD Ministerial Conference in Ottawa, Canada, in 1999: "Control ... has been tacitly transferred into the hands of tens of millions –

soon hundreds of millions – of users worldwide."[17] Power to the people. The figure below illustrates the consumer's metamorphosis over the last 40 years – from cheeping mouse to roaring lion; from nice, stupid and humble to mean, smart and demanding.

This is only the beginning. Aided by new infomediaries, people will use the Net to link up with their binary siblings – other individuals with similar cravings. They will join hands and create unions – customer unions. Just look at LetsBuyIt.com, an Internet auction-house/co-shopper, which has realized that in an age of senseless supply, those who own the demand are in charge. If you are buying a new car, how much bargaining power do you have in relation to Ford Motors, Honda, Daimler-Chrysler or even the smallest car company in the world? Not a lot. But, what if you could link up with 999 other consumers who are interested in buying the same car? Today, we can. The power is ours to use and abuse. Consumers of the world unite. Technology provides the tools. Values provide the frame.

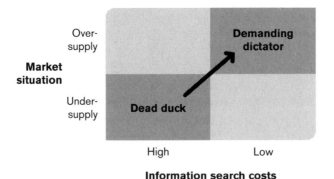

Some may assert that they're unlikely to see any of these developments in their industry. Maybe they won't but, one way or another, we will all be affected. There will be no exceptions. Your suppliers may be directly affected or your customers. If so, so will you. The force of the demanding customer or client will be felt up and down the supply chain. Universities will feel it. Soul singers will feel it. Car companies will feel it. Diamond dealers will feel it. The question of who will pay for this is not clear – maybe all firms will. The question of who will be the ultimate winner is easier – the final customer: you. We own the marketplace, lock, stock and barrel.

Competing for attention

In an age of abundance, companies have to work hard to get noticed. They are on constant tip-toe at the back of the frame trying to squeeze in. Companies are competing for a few seconds of attention. They want to be noticed in the tidal wave of information hitting everyone, everywhere and all the time. In fact, they have to be noticed.

To get noticed, they go to extremes. Excess is a business necessity. In a commercial for Miller's beer a magician makes hair grow from the armpits of the women around him. A Mercedes-Benz TV commercial in the States features a woman who so enjoys driving the car that 20 seconds into the spot she has an orgasm – from driving a car. Extreme times call for extreme measures. This is a "seen it, had it, heard it, done it, been there" type of society. Sameness sucks!

In the funky village, real competition no longer revolves around market share. We are competing for attention – *mind share and heart share.* If you cannot capture the attention of prospective customers or employees, you are out. To attract them, you need to provide experiences that are immediate, intense and instant. In an excess economy, attention is scarce. Handle it with care.

Indeed, we may well have to start paying for attention. American marketing star Seth Godin, talks about permission marketing.[18] Our contacts with those customers who don't want to drown in a tidal wave of information will be by invitation only. Yesterday, we had to pay for newspapers, phone calls and Internet connections. Today, we can get them for free, as long as we are prepared to read, listen to or watch ads. Tomorrow, we will be paid for it. We will be paid to receive a particular newspaper, to use a particular telephone company or Internet service provider. Paying for attention is the logical progression from what is already happening.

NOT ONLY IS the funky village marked by abundance and excess, the three driving forces also cause dramatic changes in time, mass and space.[19] Everything is being turned upside down and inside out. We used to do business in a world where there was plenty of time. What mattered could be seen and touched, and the game was taking place in our own back yard. No more. Now, a weird wired world is unraveling in front of our eyes. The new society is developing in real time; competition is brain-based; and the economy is globally linked.

Let us provide you with a road map for the future. The current contraction in time and expansion in space leave you standing here.

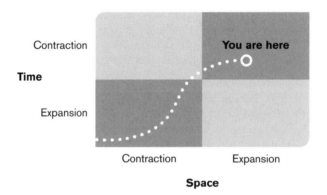

Now: the real-time society

Time is the new religion of our age. We are addicted to speed. The new society operates in real time. What once used to take three years, then took three months, then three days, then three hours, and then three minutes, now takes three seconds – approaching zero. In the real-time economy prices are set second by second, companies compete on how fast they can be to develop, make and launch products. In the real-time world we live live. This is the CNN society, instantly linked by satellite to where the action is. It is a remote control reality. If you cannot arouse my interest, if you don't appeal to my values, I will zap to someone else who can. We have to do business MTV-style. Or else, zap! The most staggering thing is that, in such a world, companies keep on publishing *annual reports*!

We are addicted to speed. We live live

The new heroes are *staminacs* – people who never seem to sleep. Recently, Bill Gates, who claims to relax quite a bit nowadays, said that, "There are days that I work 14 hours, but most days I don't work more than 12 hours. On weekends I rarely work more than 8 hours."[20] The average American now works 25 percent more than he or she did in the early 1970s.[21] It is not only Bill Gates who works unfeasibly and unhealthily long hours.

While working harder is one natural response to the funky world we find ourselves in, we seriously doubt that it is the best answer. If it were, the ultimate winners in the funky village would be people with little or no need to sleep. Instead of working harder, funky people work smarter. They do what they are really good at, maybe 100 times better. Period. Try beating that by reducing sleep.

Advances in IT have pushed us into a connected economy. And connected systems allow for real-time feedback. The dominant organization of the past may legally have been one entity, but was often better characterized as disconnected or even dismembered. It could take four weeks, or maybe sometimes four months, for the factory to hear from the salespeople at the other end of the world about booms or slumps. In the wired world supply chain feedback is instant. When something happens in Milan, the partners in New York, Montevideo and Sydney know about it immediately. Think Benetton; think sheep.

Firms, supply chains, industries, markets and even entire economies are being transformed into ultra-sensitive systems where changes anywhere are instantly registered everywhere. It's like pulling in a fishing net – no matter where you start pulling, kinetic energy will be reproduced throughout the entire net. It's like a cobweb where the spider is capable of sensing movement wherever a bug or fly has landed in the web. But remember that such sensitive systems are fragile. Every now and then they can, and do, break down or collapse.

Why, then, is real-time feedback so important? Let us just provide a few examples. In the computer industry, component costs decline by approximately 1 percent every week.[22] You don't want inventory – you want instant information. As noted earlier, the key to success is replacing information for inventory. Dell turns around its inventory 52 times per year. The equivalent number for Compaq is 13.5 and for IBM it's 9.8.[23] In which company would you buy stocks?

In addition, real-time feedback enables organizations to respond much more quickly and more accurately to customer demands. We can get better service. For instance, buying a bunch of CDs or books over the Net, we can immediately find out if they are in "stock" (at least virtually). Information on the books or CDs which people with similar taste have bought is at our fingertips. Reviews, written by other customers on the items we are planning to buy are displayed on the screen in front of us. It's the return of the local grocery store, where the dealer always knew the special interests and demands of Mrs Jones or Mr Black, though this time in digital form.

The age of auctions

The main impact of the real-time society on business is in making way for the age of auctions. In the bazaar, the fish market or at a traditional auction, prices were (and still are) always set in real time. Over time, shifts in supply and demand determine the price. Financial markets still function in that way. When we buy stocks in Motorola, Siemens, Sony, Nokia or Ericsson, we do not know exactly how much we are paying until the deal is closed. But, when we get a new mobile phone from any of these companies we know the price in advance. Why? The simple answer is that fixed prices reduce uncertainty, for both the seller and the buyer – Prozac pricing. In the funky village, however, change is a constant and instead of reducing uncertainty the emphasis will be on reducing friction – all the stuff that prevents the realization of perfect markets. In an info desert – lack of information or asymmetrically distributed information – the seller knows things that the buyer does not have a clue about, like when you buy a used car – all prevent the realization of market perfection. But in an info jungle, sooner or later, friction-free capitalism will happen.

Thanks to new technology and changes in our values, prices for any type of goods or service can once more be set instantly – as a consequence of changes in supply and demand. This is precarious pricing. We are back in the bazaar, but this time the bazaar is not necessarily limited in space. Auction Web held 330,000 on-line auctions during the first quarter of 1997.[24] And since then, the auction market has moved from being lukewarm

Real-time pricing spreads like a forest fire. We see it in the power utility industry, electronics industry, telecoms industry and airline industry.

to white hot. On-line auctioneer eBay carries 9000 products in 1086 categories and has 140,000,000 hits per week.[25] Its customers come from every corner of the globe.

Real-time pricing spreads like a forest fire. We see it in the power utility industry, electronics industry, telecoms industry and airline industry. Cathay Pacific Airways put up 387 seats of various classes for auction. The company got 15,000 bids.[26] The Swedish firm Mr Jet and the American company Price Line sell airline tickets over the Net. You enter your price, route and credit card number. If the partner airline accepts the deal, you will hear about it within an hour. In six months Price Line got bids worth some $294 million. It is now applying the same business model to hotel accommodation, and plans to add cars and mortgages to its portfolio.[27]

But real-time pricing is not necessarily tied to the Internet. The principle goes far beyond that. Some of the new vending machines that Coca-Cola distributes around the world are loaded with electronics as well as Coke. The technology enables the machine to sense the local conditions. Is it raining or is the sun shining? What is the temperature? Coca-Cola believes that local conditions are good indicators of what kind of demand there will be for a can of Coke. If the sun is shining a can may cost a dollar. If it is raining heavily, the price might go down to 50 cents.

So what are the consequences of precarious pricing for us as consumers or business managers? Some ideas might be gleaned from markets with a lot of experience in operating in real time. In financial markets, for example, you design your own risk level, cafeteria style, by using a range of instruments such as options. Let's say you are planning to buy a new motorbike. Prices are set in real time so you do not know in advance what you are going to pay. The bike you have been looking at is gaining in popularity so you fear that prices may go up. To handle the risk, you buy a bike option that two months ahead will allow you to acquire the motorcycle for a fixed price. Sixty days later, three things may have happened. The bike may cost just as much as your set price plus the cost of the option, or it may cost more or less. But what really matters is that you had an instrument that helped to design your own risk profile. You may use it or not. You may minimize or maximize your exposure to risk. You decide because you are in charge. These arrangements have worked for years in the financial world, so why can't they work when we buy a motorbike, TV or car?

Softwhere: the brain-based society

In the beginning there were products and services, things we made or things we delivered. Then money became the great bean-feast. In the 1980s doing imaginative things with money – derivatives, junk bonds, leveraged buyouts, futures – was the way to make it really big. Now, doing imaginative things with information is the road to riches. Walter Wriston, the former chairman of Citibank, was right: information about money is now more valuable than money itself.

Look at Michael Bloomberg. After running the investment bank Salomon Brothers' equity trading and technology systems, Bloomberg left the company in 1981. With a group of fellow ex-Salomon employees, Bloomberg founded Innovative Market Systems – later renamed Bloomberg. It now has annual revenues in excess of $1 billion and Bloomberg is CEO. Bloomberg's insight was that though he was successful trading with money, he could make even more when he reported on money and gave people information about money.[28]

In the information age, information is dollars. Matt Drudge is the man at the keyboards in his LA office controlling the *Drudge Report*. He styles himself as a kind of Woodward and Bernstein – the Watergate journalists – on the Internet, investigative journalist, gossip-monger, techno-newshound. Drudge will go down in history as the man who broke the Monica Lewinsky story – if the sordid tale ever reaches the history books. Drudge provides instant inside information on what is happening in the American corridors of power.

Inside information is commercial gold. Companies spend billions of dollars seeking to capture information about their customers. "Loyal customers are the spoils of the information wars and those who own the customer information own the market," says Sean Kelly, Managing Director of the Data Warehouse Network.[29]

But it is not only information about money which is more valuable than money itself. Information about products, services and just about anything that you can think of is worth more than the underlying offering. And it is not only the amount of information that is crucial, but its timeliness and accuracy. Yesterday's news on customer expectations and experiences is simply history. Today's news on customer expectations and experiences is tomorrow's profits.

Competence-based competition

Brainpower dominates modern corporations. It is their essence. We are increasingly competing on competence. A company such as Ericsson is more than 50 percent service and pure knowledge work, and at Hewlett-Packard and IBM this figure is closer to 80 and 90 percent.

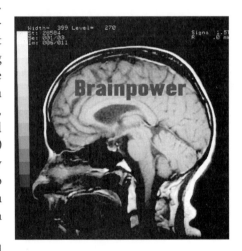

They are all being transformed, whether they like it or not, from manufacturing companies with a little service to service companies with a little manufacturing. Today, all companies are, or should be, brain-based. "We have 300 tons of brainpower ... How can we motivate our people so that those 300 tons move in a certain direction?" says Göran Lindahl, head of ABB.[30]

The changes we witnessed during the 1990s were pretty dramatic. Just study the table overleaf of the top ten companies in terms of market value in 1990 and 1998, respectively.[31]

Look, for example, at Microsoft. With only 27,000 employees, Microsoft is not the biggest company in the world, but it is still the company with the highest stock market value. In 1993, which isn't very long ago, it had 14,000 employees and a turn-over of about $3.75 billion.[32] In the same year, one of the largest corporations in the world, General Motors, had a turnover of

Company	Market value 1990 ($bn)	Company	Market value 1998 ($bn)
AT&T	119	Microsoft	318
IBM	69	General Electric	295
Industrial Bank of Japan	68	Intel	194
Shell Group	67	Merck	188
General Electric	63	Exxon	174
Exxon	60	Coca-Cola	170
Sumitomo Bank	56	Wal-Mart Stores	165
Fuji Bank	53	IBM	152
Toyota	50	Shell Group	149
Mitsui Taiyo Kobe Bank	50	Pfizer	146

$120 billion.[33] Even so, by the end of 1993, Microsoft was worth more than the whole of General Motors. Today, it is worth approximately 6.5 times as much.[34]

Think of how big General Motors is. In terms of revenue, it is still the largest company in the world ($161 billion as com-pared to Microsoft's paltry $14.4 billion). It has thousands of buildings and warehouses; it has huge sophisticated machines. It has been around a long time and in 1996 assembled 647,000 peo-ple, the population of a decent-sized city, to do its work.[35] Even without vehicle sales it would still rank among the top 30 *Fortune 500* companies.[36] Yet, Microsoft outstripped it without apparently breaking sweat. Microsoft doesn't have as many offices, warehouses or machines as General Motors. It doesn't employ as many people. In fact, the only asset of Microsoft is human imagination. It is brain-powered.

The good thing about General Motors is that it looks like a big business. With its office blocks, real estate, legions of people and huge factories, it is what we imagine big business to resemble.

Our image of corporate perfection is locked in the past – reflected in accounting procedures, management principles, generic strategies, office architecture, use of language and so on. At least the past gave you something to hold on to. The trouble with intellectual capital, brainpower, or whatever you choose to call it, is that it is ethereal and elusive. We even lack a proper language to describe knowledge. For all the checklists and models, calculating the power of the brains assembled in a room, let alone a corporation, is close to impossible. It is difficult to explain, describe and evaluate. Still, we must persevere in our pursuit of knowledge – after all, love is also difficult yet we continue to try.

Brains are now more powerful than entire countries. In 1998, Norway had roughly $17 billion in cash in the country's oil foundation.[37] This is the dividend from 30 years of oil production in the North Sea. Thirty years of hard work. Think of the thousands of oil workers with the gusty North Sea winds blowing in their faces, rain running down the back of their necks, spending weeks away from their families and friends. It is a huge amount of money, carefully set aside as a kind of national pension fund to ensure that a small country remains a wealthy country. However, it is not as huge as the market valuation of amazon.com, the Internet bookstore started in the summer of 1995 and which, after four years of doing business, had not made a single dime in profits. As of May 1999, amazon.com was valued at $23 billion, a little more than half of Yahoo ($34.5 billion).[38] A gang of youthful nerds has outstripped the oil workers. Keep on drilling.

If you want proof of the power of the human brain think of what would happen to Microsoft if William Gates III suddenly announced he had had enough and was going to take up golf and dabble in investing like his colleague Paul Allen did. Microsoft would probably struggle to survive. A multi-billion-dollar company is forever being held at ransom. "We are always 18 months away from failure," says Bill Gates. If Microsoft is perpetually teetering on the abyss what hope can there be for the rest of us?

The new hard currency is information. As Nicholas Negroponte of MIT's Media Lab puts it: "We are moving from a world of atoms into one of bits."[39] We are moving from brawn to brain, from hired hands to hired heads. Competition is about kilobytes, not kilograms.

Yet, we are stuck in the world of atoms. We continue to measure atoms as if they were still the most important things in life. The trade agreement GATT is mainly about atoms – about how many tons of a certain good we can move from one geographical location to another. While information travels across borders at the speed of light, few politicians seem to be that bothered. Our balance sheets are about atoms – machines, buildings, etc. – but do we really capture the most critical assets by measuring that stuff?

We are talking about a major mind-shift. And even some of those who sing the "softwhere" gospel most loudly must repent. Recently, a good friend of ours left her position at one of the most renowned consulting companies in the world. She was neither the first to leave the company, nor the last. In fact, consultant after consultant was leaving the firm – particularly female consultants. If they had stayed with the organization for another 10 years, they would probably have been worth at least $2 million each in future earnings. Yet, management did close to nothing to find out why so many left. A month later, the firm threw an internal office party. Someone left with a $200 Italian lamp. The following day, the head of the organization sent an e-mail to all employees explaining that if the lamp was not immediately returned, he would personally contact the police. It seems that even at one of the best-respected consulting companies in the world, $200 worth of stuff is still more valuable than tens of millions of dollars worth of fluff.

In our new age, being elusive is good. If you can touch something, it is probably not worth a great deal. What is valuable at Volvo, the car manufacturer that was recently acquired by Ford Motors, you cannot touch. The manufacturing facilities are not worth a great deal and the company's headquarters and the warehouse in Holland are nothing more than real estate. What is valuable is the intangible – the Volvo brand, the relationships, the knowledge that exists within the company, the concepts, and ideas. Ford had to pay $6.45 billion for all this – a little more than what 4 percent of America Online, or AOL ($149.8 billion) would have cost them.[40] Dealers in and of atoms are in for some pretty tough times.

If you can touch something, it is probably not worth a great deal.

The value of intangibles affects every business and every aspect of our society and personal lives.

Take a human being, break him or her down to the smallest of components – atoms. Bring that stuff to the commodities market in Chicago and try to sell it – if you are lucky you will get two bucks.[41] Instead, reassemble the person. Call him Jerry Seinfeld and ask for an annual salary of more than $100 million.

Take some water, add sugar, carbonate it, and pour it into a can. The cost is probably less than a quarter. Write Coca-Cola on the can and you can charge a dollar.

Take a cardboard box, a small booklet and a CD-ROM. Together it is probably worth some $20. Write Lotus Notes on it and you can charge $499.

Take a cheap fabric, make a pair of pants using a 100-year-old design and you might struggle to make a fortune. Production cost: around $7.[42] Put the name Levi's on it and you can charge $50. In the brain-based society, perception is all; the intangible is made real by the shrill sound of cash registers. In the brand-based society, Bacardi-Martini paid £1.5 billion ($2.4 billion) for Dewar's 4 distilleries, 49 employees and a 15-year supplier contract. The company also got the White Label scotch whisky, Bombay Gin and Bombay Sapphire Gin brand names.[43] Strange? Maybe not if you consider the list of some of the most valuable brands in the world.[44]

No wonder that Gerhard Pichtesrieder, former CEO at BMW, reflected that he was not really the one who ran the company. He had someone on top of him. The BMW brand on top of the headquarters building, and its heavy weight of history, was the company's real leader.

Intelligence and intangibles go hand in hand. But intangibles cost. God does not hand out great brands. Great brands are created – and it takes time. With the exception of Absolut Vodka, how many hot, new liquor brands are you aware of? Quite often the information cost – what it takes to attract the interest of oversupplied and increasingly demanding customers – surpasses the actual costs of producing the customer offering. Just think of Coke, Metallica, Gap, Madonna, Prada, or Tiger Woods.

Brand	Brand value ($ billion)
Coca-Cola	47.99
Marlboro	47.64
IBM	23.70
McDonalds	19.94
Disney	17.07
Sony	14.46
Kodak	14.44
Intel	13.27
Gillette	11.99
Budweiser	11.99

Everywhere: the globally linked society

The reality is that we all live in a borderless world. Most of us are so used to the idea of internationalization that we take it for granted. Look at the clothes you are wearing. As we write, one of us is wearing a suit from Germany, shoes from Italy, a shirt from Canada, and the other is in a pair of pants from the US and a Belgian T-shirt, wearing glasses from Japan. You might think that we cheated – putting on our global costumes in preparation – but we swear to you (on the embalmed body of Lenin) that we are just wearing what everyone else is wearing, albeit only in black. Look around. How many nations do your clothes originate from? We bet that, unless you are currently in bed, you would get into serious trouble by taking off all the clothes not made in your home country.

On the other hand, "Made in the USA" is increasingly meaningless. So, too, is "Made in Japan" or "Made in Swaziland". Robert Reich tells the story of how a few years back GM's Pontiac LeMans was made from components from the US ($8000), South Korea ($6000), Japan ($3500), Germany ($1500), and others ($1000).[45] Similarly, the Volvo 850 car produced in Ghent, Belgium, had only 25 percent Swedish components. Was the 850 a Swedish car? The Finnish company Nokia has labs in Scandinavia, Japan, Hong Kong, Germany, Australia, the UK and the US. It sends its people to Venice Beach in LA and Kings Road in London to pick up the latest fashion signals. Are its products Finnish? By 1998, non-Swedes owned around 35 percent of companies on the Stockholm Stock Exchange and, in the case of Ericsson, the figure was close to 50 percent. If the nation state is now a meaningless unit of measurement, attribution to a particular nation is also redundant. Interestingly, it is the older generation that remains loyal to nationally produced goods. The British buy British, the French buy French and the Americans buy American out of long-held habit. It is an expression of patriotism. The young couldn't care less. Today, it's made by BMW, made by Nokia, made by Alessi, made by Sony. What matters is who – not where. It's *made by* – not *made in.*

Globalization is no longer a theory. It affects nation states, firms, products, services, and individuals. And it affects them now, simultaneously. Local used to be the norm and international the exception. Business schools used to have special departments for international business. Now, one small department for local business is more appropriate. Why do governments have separate Ministries of Foreign Affairs when most governmental affairs are international? The new institutions cut across geographical boundaries. There are megastates, such as the EU, APEC, NAFTA; multinational firms that are legally local, but operatively global; global products such as Coca-Cola and the Big Mac; global super-specialists; and a host of global musicians, consultants, chefs, researchers, actors, and many more.

True internationalization – rather than the false alarms we have had in the past – means that a tailor in Wuhan, China is genuinely competing with one in Berlin. There is techno-economic parity – knowledge dissemination means that people in the West no longer have knowledge monopolies so the tailor in Wuhan can quickly have access to the same technology as the tailor in Berlin. The spirit of capitalism is on the move. It has been since it left Europe at the end of the nineteenth century to pay a visit to the USA. Then, it kept going West to end up in the Far East. It is still moving westwards, waving its magic wand over China and the former USSR. The new reality is developing everywhere. The new economy is multi-centric.

What matters is who – not where. It's *made by* – not *made in.*

The Far West

Look West. Look to the Far West because that it where the future is unraveling. Many more new jobs are created in the US than in

Europe. But, the US economy is peculiar in that only certain regions, industries, and companies are extremely dynamic. California, not surprisingly, is one of the clusters of growth. This is a strange place where 40 percent of the population never use knives and forks for eating, preferring to eat with their hands while standing up.[46] So, international competition seems to be a battle between those who eat with sticks, those who use a knife and a fork, and the supposed sophisticates who merely use their hands. They may use their hands for eating, but their heads drive the economy.

This is a bits, tits and ass economy – Sillywood (Silicon Valley + Hollywood) rules and tittytainment is the name of the game. Much of what is interesting in the US, at least from a business perspective, is linked to the expanding entertainment cluster. While more films are produced by the European Union countries combined than by the United States, the US films have a 75 percent market share in Western Europe.[47] Don't be fooled, however. Entertainment does not only mean Arnold Schwarzenegger movies or Madonna CDs. Entertainment also means high-tech. Just think of SiliconGraphics and Mickey Mouse. Films, music, electronic toys, videos and computer games merge with all aspects of IT – hardware and software, telecommunications, the Net and so on – into a highly potent brew.

The US economy leads the way in creating an information society. For instance, the US spends 4 percent of its GDP on IT, while Japan spends only 2 percent.[48] The US economy is getting softer by the hour. Silicon Valley companies are now valued at four times those of Detroit; and their value almost equals that of the entire French stock market.[49] Palo Alto, California, a place formerly known for its bowel-friendly delicious prunes and raisins, is now home to 7000 electronics and software firms.[50] Within the next 24 hours or so, 62 newly made US dollar millionaires will be out having fun in the warm Californian sun.[51]

Computer and semiconductor companies account for a staggering 45 percent of US growth.[52] What's good for General Motors increasingly does not appear to be good for America.

The Far East

Nevertheless, it would be wrong to say that the future is only developing in the Far West. The Far East has exploded in economic growth during the last 10 to 20 years. During the eighteenth century it took Great Britain some 60 years to double its GDP, says Professor Jeffrey D. Sachs of Harvard University. Sachs notes that 100 years later, Japan managed to do it in half that time. Recently, South Korea did it in 11 years. Back in 1960, the standard of living for the average Japanese citizen was ⅛ of that of an American.[53] Economically, South Korea was at the same level as Sudan, and Taiwan equaled Zaire in GDP per capita terms.[54] Before the current crisis, the World Bank estimated that as much as 50 percent of future worldwide growth during the next decades would be located in Southeast Asia.[55]

The Far East comes with a positive yearning for education. Some time ago, kids from all around the world were asked whether or not going to school was one of their favorite activities? In China 34 percent said that it was. In Japan 28 percent agreed. The equivalent number for the US was 18 percent.[56]

Even so, the magnitude of the shift remains underestimated. The West is in denial. Some people believe that the recent economic crisis in the Far East has finally proven them right. Certain people still argue that most of these countries produce cheap electronic gadgets and plastic toys. Such claims are easily rebutted. A Merrill Lynch study shows that in places, such as Singapore, Hong Kong, and Taiwan, more than 60 percent of GDP stems from service-related activities. Many of these economies are already knowledge-based. We were recently told that a country like Singapore – once described by author William Gibson as "Disneyland with the death penalty" – spends 25 percent of its GDP on education, research and development. We think those guys have a plan. But of course, Singapore could be wrong. What if we are not going through a revolution? What if knowledge isn't going to be a key asset in the future? Dream on.

In Southeast Asia, much of the manufacturing is now carried out in China – a country that annually produces 350,000 engineers with an average monthly salary of slightly above $100. China has more high-school graduates than America (by a couple of hundred million) and includes 413.7 million people who are under 20.[57] The Chinese are young, educated and greedy. Chinese people are almost like us: while we want to *get* rich they want to *be* rich. A recent survey showed that some 66 percent of the Chinese population have this as their prime driving force. A paltry 4 percent want to continue the great Communist revolution.[58] Until the early nineteenth century the Chinese economy was the largest economy in the world. If growth continues for the next few years, in 2010 it will have regained its position as the dominant economy on planet Earth.

Naturally, the impact of Asian competition will change over the coming years. Pure brute force competition will be complemented by brain force competition. We can probably learn a great deal from the evolution of Japan as an industrial power. In the beginning, the Japanese made things that were cheaper; the West dismissed them as inexpensive plastic crap. Then, they progressed to make things that were also better. The West made the mistake of assuming the old joke applied. It didn't. As the Japanese killed off most Western electronics companies and slaughtered virtually all the automotive companies, Westerners almost choked on their laughs. Malicious pleasure over the Asian crisis may be similarly short-lived as billions of brains start banging on the door to the West. Just wait, after pleasure comes pressure.

The Close(d) East

Traveling to the Far West or Far East is not enough. The future is also in the Close(d) East. Some of these economies have undergone tremendous changes since the fall of the Berlin Wall in 1989. A few years ago, the Hungarian Economic Minister gave a speech to a group of journalists in which he explained why Communism fell. He provided a long and detailed macroeconomic explanation. When he was done his wife, who happens to be one of Hungary's many new entrepreneurs, rose from her chair and said, "I'm not sure I understand what my husband just told you, but I will tell you, my friends and I want to go shopping."[59]

We can look at the Close(d) East using three complementary perspectives.

1 For some companies, Eastern Europe is an enormous mess – no infrastructure, organized crime, a different mentality, etc.
2 For others Eastern Europe is a gigantic output market – Mercedes sells a lot of luxury cars in Moscow.
3 These countries make up a tremendous input market – there is a mega brain-sale in these countries, particularly of people who used to work in the defense industry.

It is interesting that some Russian companies no longer hire people from the West because, they say, Westerners are not capitalist enough. They argue that the comfortable citizens of the West are not prepared to work as long hours, as hard and to bend the rules as much when this is necessary. The eastern Europeans remain hungry.

Near Here

Unexpected things are happening in Western Europe too. Who would have thought that one of the fastest-growing companies in the software industry – the funkiest of industries – would be German and called SAP? Where did Nokia – maker of the sexiest and most stylish mobile phones on the market – come from? Today, Finland exports more electronics than forestry products.[60] The Finns also have more Internet hosts per capita than any other country.[61] Ten years ago, who would have anticipated that three of the world's hottest airlines would be British? Now, just look at easyJet, Virgin and Ryan Air. And just how many would have predicted that two of the greatest and fastest-growing Web designers would be Swedish – home of some of the most brawny companies around. Now Sweden has Icon Medialab and

SprayRazorfish and can even boast that it is the third largest music exporter in the world.

Europe offers a number of multicultural role models, from soccer teams to entire countries. Some of the most thriving and international of companies are headquartered in multi-ethnic and multireligious Switzerland. Companies such as Nestlé, Ciba Geigy and ABB appear to handle diversity more easily and positively than others in Europe. ABB's supervisory board of eight includes four nationalities, and its executive committee goes one further with five. Its former chief executive Percy Barnevik argues that: "Competence is the key selection criterion, not passport." Other multinationals are similarly diverse as they discover the twin challenges of globalization and teamwork. After its merger, the medical/biotech company SmithKline Beecham boasted a management group of 13 that included 7 nationalities. Europe strikes back.

Etc.

We could go on and on. The economy is growing in a multitude of places. There is no longer a single center of gravity; there are many. The Western project – a little pink house with a white fence, a reliable car, a good-looking wife or husband, nice kids, an annual summer vacation to the Mediterranean or the Caribbean, and a decent, steady job – is no longer challenged by only 200 million people. It is no longer just Japan breathing down Western necks. Today, 3000 million people want to **3000 million people want to have what most Westerners already have – and they want it now.** have what most Westerners already have – and they want it now. And, trust us, they won't say please. Frightening? On the contrary. This is the greatest business opportunity of the new millennium. The positive scenario is, of course, that these 3 billion individuals will all soon be potential customers.

But the funky village is not only global – it is globally linked. Remember the fishnet and the cobweb – changes spread and can be felt everywhere. A market economy is not a zero-sum game. If people in Asia suffer from a recession, that does not improve the standard of living for people in the West, in anything but relative terms. If growth in the US economy skyrockets, that's not bad news for anyone on this planet. We are building the international interlinked society together. The funky village means more competition, but it also means more opportunities – opportunities to find new customers, suppliers, partners, experts, and friends. The price for not being linked, however, is extremely high. Give Saddam Hussein or Slobodan Milosevic a call and they will tell you.

Leaders and laggards

Clearly, not all regions are growing at the same rate. According to the World Bank's economic experts, people in fast-growing economies simply work harder, study harder and save more. Economic success and progress is about simple things: working, studying and saving – no magic powder or wand will do the trick.

During the 1990s, the US economy regained its position as No. 1. We can see this, for instance, in terms of the share of world stock market value represented by Japanese and US companies.[62]

Five years ago the Asians, and particularly Japan, seemed unstoppable, but in the run up to the new millennium many of these economies came to a grinding halt. What happened? Should we be surprised? The short answer is no. In the last phase of the industrial era, we played a game focused on efficiency, exploitation and incremental improvements, mass-production, one more product, exactly like the last one, then one more – only slightly better. Those who succeeded were wizards at perfecting the known.[63] They excelled at doing things right.

In the funky village, the game revolves around effectiveness, creation and revolutionary changes, new customer offerings,

Share of world stock market value		
Year	Japan	The United States
1990	41.5%	31.0%
1998	10.4%	53.2%

being completely different, surprising people, providing amazing stuff. Success comes from exploring the unknown and getting it roughly right.

Players with different profiles will dominate throughout the lifecycle of any era. In the funky village, there is one region characterized by highly individualistic values. It has institutions that allow for a fluid, temporary and mobile labor market. A region that accepts uncertainty and is a creator of new technology – the United States. So we should not be surprised that American firms now dominate at the beginning of this new era – particularly when collectivism, lifetime employment, uncertainty reduction and the assimilation, rather than the creation, of new technology mark one of the main contenders – Japan.[64]

It will not necessarily remain the case. America's long boom is not written in tablets of stone. Its dominance may not end right away, but it will certainly be challenged. Increased globalization and value-fusion will have their say. Many people are no longer trapped by geography. Certain Japanese, Danish or Portuguese people are more individualistic creators and uncertainty embracers than the typical American is. The world is now their stage. They are free to exercise their right to choose. And choices they will make. So, we should expect faster and unexpected comebacks as these individuals pick up signals and ideas from one region and transplant them to another. In a placeless society, individuals and organizations with many homes should not be confused with nation states that cannot be cut loose and shipped off somewhere else. Once again, *who* appears more important than *where*.

Results from the third international math and science study (TIMSS), in which the knowledge of 13-year-olds from around the world is measured, also make you wonder about how long the US can stay ahead.[65]

In a brain-based economy, can American dominance prevail, when on average its youngsters are playing in the minor league? A more critical question, however, is whether or not the average is at all interesting. If the funky people, given a specific task, really happen to be 100 times smarter than the rest, isn't the average score just as interesting as geographical borders, public service TV, brawn-based companies and old Albanian cartoons?

Maths	Score	Science	Score
1. Singapore	643	1. Singapore	607
2. South Korea	607	2. Czech Republic	574
3. Japan	605	3. Japan	571
4. Hong Kong	588	4. South Korea	565
5. Belgium	565	5. Bulgaria	565
28. United States	500	17. United States	534

Then there is the question of Europe. If the US and Japan (and much of the rest of Asia for that matter) provide the two extremes – is Europe stuck in the middle or can it combine the best of both worlds? Of one thing we can be sure, if Europe is to make the best of all possible worlds it has to utilize the very diversity that has ignited several wars within it during the twentieth century.

Particularly in the United States, diversity is a hot topic. Companies have diversity initiatives backed by expensive advertising campaigns as they fall over themselves to be perceived as politically correct. The difference in the US is that diversity is largely a matter of color. In Europe, it is a matter of culture.[66] The new melting pot is Europe.

Europeans typically live in countries where 15 to 25 percent of people have foreign backgrounds. The mix is everything. There are no longer any closed, homogeneous, sheltered societies. Living alongside people with different values and value systems is now a fact of life. Of course, all is not sweetness and light. Some societies are more nationalistic than others. No one ever said that living together would be without tension. The result is that Europe has a potential diversity advantage – an advantage in that diversity is the mother of creativity, invention and progress. But are the Europeans sitting on top of a powder keg or a melting pot? Europe has a long history of hostility and rivalry. Its people are used to living in disunity. Is this an asset or a liability? According to the German academic Jurgen Habermas, Europe's heritage definitely works to its advantage when trying to develop the means of handling disunity – a supranational democracy; the European Union. Practice makes perfect.

Still, recent developments in the Balkans make even the most optimistic person think twice about the dangers of diversity. But remember, what is is. Europe is – and has been for centuries – heterogeneous in race, religion, and every conceivable dimension. Diversity *per se* is not necessarily good or bad – it just is. Diversity becomes what we make of it. Europe does not necessarily need more or less diversity. Europe needs to make up its mind what to do with it. Europe needs a dream, an idea, a new manifesto – words and action. Europeans need to make up their minds as to how to maximize the potential of its heterogeneous population by using advances in technology, institutions and values. Or else, the other players in the funky village will shape Europe's destiny.

THERE ARE NOT only changes in time, space and mass. Entering the age of abundance, the world is metamorphosing, taking on new and unclear shapes. Things are drifting, torn apart and recombined in unconventional ways – *panta rei* – to create a blurred, fragmented and hyphenated world.

Our society is left in a state of confusion. Empowered individuals, talent holders, individuals who have the power of choice, inhabit this state of confusion. They are people who are free to know, go, do and be whoever they want to be.[67] These individuals, who exercise their right to choose, are creating this age of "anarchy". They tear down walls and undermine traditional bases of power. They take control over their education, careers and lives. They initiate system-wide changes that transform the world into a hyper-pluralistic place.

Yesterday, strong centers of power dominated society and our lives. In the 1848 Manifesto of the Communist Party, the authors wrote that the aim was to create a society: "In which industrial production is no longer directed by individual factory owners, competing against one another, but by the whole of society according to a fixed plan and according to the needs of all." This was the extreme of social engineering with all its assumptions of predictability, stability and control. Driven by an overall vision of the good life, it was just a matter of getting the central plan, structures and systems right. Conservative politicians, capitalists and business managers in the West may have laughed at these utopian aspirations, but were their visions really any better?

We built our own huge, monolithical and centrally planned structures. Some of them we called corporations. A little more than 30 years ago Harvard economist and advisor to John F. Kennedy, John Kenneth Galbraith, admitted that: "We have an economic system which, whatever its formal ideological billing, is in substantial part a planned economy. Initiative in deciding what is to be produced comes not from the sovereign consumer ... Rather it comes from the great producing organization which reaches forward to control the market that it is presumed to serve."[68] Once again, it was just a matter of getting the structures, systems and strategies – the great master plan – right. In capitalism and Communism alike, there were elements of central planning – in political, social and economic terms. Some made the decisions and the others obeyed, or were at least told to obey.

If the Old World was a well-structured place filled with castrated individuals, the reality of our times is an unstructured world populated by capable individuals (and some who still seem to prefer eunuch-like uncertainty reduction). Termites have been let loose within our structures and are running amok.

Today, as the poet William Butler Yeats once wrote, the center cannot hold. Equipped with new technologies and values, entrepreneurial individuals challenge the conventional institutions and purveyors of power. Note that it is not technology, institutions or values that create the New World. The changes, or elements of confusion that we are experiencing, are caused by individuals who no longer accept being told what to know and do, where to go and who to be.

The reality of our times is an unstructured world populated by capable individuals.

But, what may be interpreted as chaos on the societal level is anything but chaotic to these individuals. It is only natural. We do not have to look further than ourselves. Most people do not expect male assistant professors at a prestigious business school to wear black leather pants, shave their heads, do gigs, listen to The Prodigy CDs, take half a year of paternity leave and so on. But we do, because we feel like it. Paradoxically, harmonious (?) individuals striving to fulfill their own personal dreams create what some may deem to be a disharmonious society. Disharmonious or not, you can't argue with the fact that it is different. What is is.

The blurred society

In the blurred society traditional divides are becoming ever more disordered. Barriers are disappearing and things are floating. We created and used our traditional structures to sort stuff into neat little piles of similar elements. By categorizing things we reduced uncertainty. Some were sellers, others buyers. We all agreed on that. Some were banks and others insurance companies. Nothing strange about that. Some were wholesalers and others retailers. Some were liberals and others socialists. Some studied and others worked. Our world was like a deck of cards and we had agreed upon (or been told to use) only one principle for sorting the cards.

Now, the three drivers of change open up possibilities for creative people to re-structure, re-sort and re-classify basically every

Where does it end, where does it begin?

little aspect of our socio-economic landscape. Nothing is given. The entire pack of cards is in the air. Previously, we have talked about blurring geographical and moral boundaries, but the effects can also be seen in a variety of other phenomena.

Industries are blurring. Given that entry barriers are falling as a consequence of internationalization, deregulation and digitization, it is easier for firms to make crossovers. Companies using a new logic enter industry after industry, because to them traditional industrial boundaries make little or no sense. On the surface, they may look like old conglomerates, but in reality they are distinctively different. The underlying idea is that their *capabilities*, not their physical resources, can be used to compete in several industries. Much of the tangible stuff is left to suppliers from all over the world. Just look at the likes of Lego, Virgin or Harley-Davidson. In addition, by focusing more on the needs of the demanding customer, rather than the actual product offering and historical definitions, companies that used to be regarded as players in different industries are beginning to compete. Today, who can tell a bank from an insurance company? They basically provide the same kind of service. From the point of view of the hard-to-please consumer, traditional distinctions are absolutely meaningless. They just want funky business.

Relationships between companies are blurring. If we actually start paying our customers for their attention, just who is the customer? Right now, sellers are also buyers and buyers are sellers. Consider the case of Swedish retailer IKEA. The company sits in the middle of a web of relationships. It has outsourced assembly to customers who want to save a buck or two hundred. In effect, the customers are also suppliers. IKEA has left component manufacturing to grateful suppliers who are also customers, gaining access to databases and expert advice. Conclusion: it is getting increasingly difficult to decide whom to invite to the company's annual Christmas party. Where does the firm end, and where does it begin? The legal boundaries are becoming less relevant and less important. Our relationship to one and the same organization may well simultaneously contain elements of competition, cooperation, supplying and buying – Fuji-Kodak, GM-Toyota, Dell-IBM, Sony-Philips. The business environment is now a promiscuous place.

Production and consumption merge into *prosumption*.[69] One of us recently bought a new Volvo car. He initiated the process by producing a list of specifications: color, engine, stereo, upholstery, finance deal, etc. Then, Volvo took this list of specs to produce the car that he and his family wanted to consume. Buyers and sellers work together in a circular process. IT opens up opportunities for even more prosumption. Just consider the active part we take when dealing with amazon.com – providing implicit input about demand and the mix of books, allowing it to track virtual shopping baskets and give tips, or more explicitly in co-creating competitiveness by sending in feedback or book reviews. The company even regularly pays $1000 (in book vouchers) to the best amateur critic.

Products and services are also blurring. It is now more accurate to talk about *provices* and *serducts*, as you can hardly separate the two.[70] Atoms and bits co-exist in most modern customer offerings. Think of the finance deals accompanying most capital goods we buy (or lease). Think of the pre-packaged "products" we are offered from financial institutions. Is a Happy Meal at McDonalds a service or a product? It is both.

The traditional distinction between leisure and work is becoming increasingly blurred. If 70 to 80 percent of the work that people perform in a modern organization is done by way of their intellects is not work a process that goes on continually – 168 hours per week? People do not stop thinking just because they leave the office. Many people even work while sleeping. Ideas are processed in our dreams. This development also makes the classical distinction between home and office less relevant. In the blurred society, work is no longer a place – it is an activity.[71]

Etc. Etc. Everywhere we look, we see blur – East-West, Men-Women, Structure-Process, Right-Wrong. And we experience blur at multiple levels – society, organizations and individuals. But remember, things look blurred only to those stuck in the logic of the past. To those who welcome the funky village there is nothing particularly mysterious about this trend. It is a fact of life. These entrepreneurial individuals and organizations look upon the changes they initiate as restructuring and innovation rather than chaos and confusion.

The fragmented society

Out of focus it may be, but our world is also being torn apart. It is fragmenting. This, perhaps not surprisingly, is generally regarded as a bad thing. This is not necessarily true – especially not from the point of view of the individual. Fragmentation is largely caused by our wish to belong to and associate with a certain group of people – our desire not to be a commodity, standardized and exactly like the others. If people indeed have been given the power of choice we should not be surprised (or ashamed) that they make different choices.

Society has always been fragmented. But, in the funky village, fundamentally new divides are created. In the not so distant past, we were separated along the lines of blood and proximity. The manuscript for what role we were supposed to play was largely determined by our family and geography. We could act only within neatly defined boundaries and parameters that told us who we were and what to expect of life. Now, new factors come into play. Depending on the level of abstraction, we can spot at least three different types of increased fragmentation.

Polarization

Polarization is increasing. Some 300 years ago, wealth was a question of controlling land. Then capital became the thing. No more.

The first of the new apartheids is education. There is a growing gap between the educated and the uneducated. These are the new classes, and this is the new class society. Without unique skills, you are totally exchangeable, and therefore also in direct competition with more than two billion Chinese and Indians. The gap between the employed and the unemployed is increasing. Hardly surprisingly, the rich are getting richer, and the poor poorer. We are on our way toward a ⅔ or ¾ type of society in which a large proportion of people are constantly losing ground.

At a global level there is a growing gap between North and South – 80 percent of all consumption is made by 20 percent of the population on planet Earth. It is a global village with exceptions. Unfortunately, from a strictly economic perspective, we could sink the African continent (with the exception of South Africa) in the Atlantic Ocean and the world economy would hardly be affected.

We see a similar development between old and young. Most young people certainly don't want to end up like their parents, having a steady job in a big organization where you get a gold watch and a pat on the back after 40 years of loyal service. That, to a large extent, is human nature. But, in terms of skills the differences between young and old people have never been as great.

The second new apartheid is an IT one – and it is binary. Percy Barnevik sometimes says that at ABB there are two kinds of people – AC and BC – after computers and before computers. Those under 25 have not experienced an IT revolution, but an evolution. They were born with it. To many of them the personal computer is the most natural thing in the world. Either you're in or you're out. These young individuals pose new and different questions of life and work. They want to change the very definition of their jobs. Instead of living to work, they work to live.

Even so, there are still people who say that values never really change, and that things stay the same. This can be easily disproved: just take a look at the cover of a 1960s *Playboy* and compare it to a current front page of *Elle* or *Cosmopolitan*.

Tribalization

Many of us grew up in a world in which geography mattered and proximity ruled. If you were born in Nice, there was an extremely strong likelihood that you would be raised in Nice, go to school in Nice, get a job in Nice, meet your spouse (who also came from Nice) in Nice, buy a house in Nice, have kids in Nice, retire to Nice, die in Nice and finally be buried in Nice. Maybe, if you were really adventurous and could afford it, you would go to the Alps on vacation every now and then. Our old society was geographically structured and so were the tribes. We had the Sydney tribe, the Stuttgart tribe and the Stockholm tribe.

Then forces of funk reshaped our world. The funky village is biographically structured. The new tribes are global. They develop with the people who are relevant to you, no matter where they are. Global *blood-based* tribes have been around for centuries – the Jewish tribe and overseas Chinese. Now, we also see *attitude-based* and *competence-based* tribes. Thanks to globalization and digitization place is no longer relevant. What are Greenpeace, Amnesty International, hell's angels or hip-hoppers

Biographical tribes

but global biographical tribes made up of people from anywhere in the world? The same goes for MBAs, architects, hackers, engineers and musicians who draw their skills (and attitudes) from global communities. These tribes have their own languages, dress codes, signs, symbols, totems and rituals.

The tribal pioneers are often found in groups considered outcasts and marginal in the geographically structured world. They are people who had great difficulties in finding enough like-minded people in their own neck of the woods. They were basically forced to search globally in pursuit of their tribe. Perhaps, we should all learn from the gay community, the Mafia, illicit drug-traders, masochists and the eco-tribe, because in the funky village your tribe is determined by biography not geography, by choice rather than proximity.

Individualization

If we take this trend one step further, we face total fragmentation and extreme individualization. The good news is that the opportunities for self-realization have never been as great. In principle, we can all become as unique as our own fingerprints, as unique as we were really meant to be. The pundits claim that we are entering a ME, ME, ME type of world – the selfish society, an egocentric economy. But individualism does not necessarily imply egoism. It has more to do with self-realization – being a whole person. For better or for worse, each individual becomes a microcosm of supply and demand in a global market.

Loyalty, in this environment, is recast. The global knowledge worker, part of the new élite, is loyal to himself or herself and the tribe, rather than the (temporary) employer. In a casino-loyal economy these people will only link up and cooperate with those who will prove beneficial to them. They will form global tribes that will roam the world as "overnight armies of intellectual mercenaries", as MIT's Thomas Malone puts it. They will buy only from those organizations that are compatible with the values of their own tribe – those who share the same vibe.

From a business point of view it is crucial to understand that the group of "lead customers", those who represent the needs and requirements of consumers in the future, will not only consist of knowledge workers and the rich.[72] Men and women with a degree in science, an MBA, and a promising career may consume more than the rest of the population. But, more consumption does not necessarily imply more foresight or insight. Quality does not follow from quantity.

We were all brought up with the notion that patient, cautious acquisition was the way to gradually build a better life. Today, consumers will often be drawn from the downwardly noble – people who may not have all the money in the world, but spend every single cent on one thing.[73] They focus on acquiring the symbols that are critical to their tribe or themselves. They sacrifice everything to get the latest and funkiest mountain bike,

Extreme diversity

travelling experience, surfboard, bottle of wine (perhaps not the latest one in this case), DVD player, yoga class, or whatever. This is where we should look if we want a glimpse of the future, not to those who excel in average spending capability.

Not everyone will join the individualistic acquisition frenzy. Some will get lost in the funky village. Not because they do not fit in, but because they will exercise their right to say no. And some will choose to deny what is happening. These groups will undoubtedly fight back through extreme localization and increased hostility against IT, dissidents and the overall fusion in values. Reactionaries can be found in any camp – businesspeople and executives who still believe in management by fear, neo-Nazis and Fascists who believe races should be kept apart; men who claim that women are not interested in making careers, politicians who think and act as if markets have not been deregulated.

Change is not friction-free – many of those in command of the present system will fight back. The old does not give in to the new without resistance. Capitalism and democracy now threaten the Communist economy of China. So what do the leaders in Beijing do? Do they shift institutions *en masse?* No. They start making adjustments to the existing institutions by introducing elements of the market economy. Similarly, values have changed so that the likes of divorce, one-parent families, and homosexual relationships are accepted. These are value-based innovations that created benefits for many who felt uneasy with the previous norms. Then, disciples of orthodoxy strike back. Just look at the ultra-conservative moral right in the US.

The principles underlying these wide-ranging examples are the same. Change is not automatic – it must be created by individual entrepreneurs.

The hy-phe-na-ted society

The future also brings more fusion. Welcome to *hyphe-nation* – a cut and paste culture. If there is a surplus of basically everything that we can imagine, the natural way for people and organizations to escape this excess is to combine things in novel ways. And the weirder the combination, the more unique the result. The realities of our times call for mixing the existing into something exciting – just look at edu-tainment, caffe-latte, corporate-university, info-tainment, distance-learning, visual-ergonomic, TV-dinners, info-com, psycho-linguistics, bio-tech, e-mail, anti-bacterial-clothes, gin-tonic and so on. Some of these phenomena are so new that we do not yet have any names for them – food with added vitamins or even food combined with drugs. But they do exist.

And hyphenation is omnipresent. You see it in business. Products are increasingly turned into multi-technology offerings – such as Kodak's photo-disk or Sony's digital Mavica.[74] A firm such as Canon combines chemistry, electronics, and software. For a car company like BMW, innovation is a question of blending mechanics with electronics, design and finance skills. L'Oréal mixes pharmaceuticals and fashion when developing its fragrances and lotions. Companies try to capture the attention of demanding customers by offering something more, something new, something surprising.

You see it in music. A hit record in the 1950s was just a song. A current hit requires a song, a look, a video, and a demon producer. How else can we explain the success of the Spice Girls? You see it in the makeup of organizations. In Silicon Valley companies, for instance, traditional "minority groups" such as women, immigrants, and youngsters are dramatically over-represented compared to their status in traditional US firms. You see it in art. German painter Michel Majerus combines Watteau with Warhol and Walt Disney cartoons. American artist Clay Ketter mixes painting with construction materials and IKEA kitchen cabinets. We see it in architecture, food, sports, education, and healthcare. We see it everywhere.

Some will say that hyphenation is the ultimate proof of our lack of imagination. Others suggest that as everything that ever will be invented has been invented, the only way forward is to combine what is already there. The result of both views is that we end up living in an ultra-boring post-modern society.

The other interpretation of hyphenation is that variation in itself breeds even more variation. If certain individuals or companies combine a and b into c, c can then be used to find new combinations with d, e, f and so on. Once it gets going, variation by its very nature increases exponentially.

It is also vital to keep in mind that hyphenation at its best does not mean addition but multiplication – the value created must be more than the sum of the parts combined. In other words, pro-

The natural way for people and organizations to escape this excess is to combine things in novel ways.

fitable hyphenation requires combining things in such a way that extra value is created. At the same time it needs to be difficult for the customer to unbundle the offering. Because if the customer can easily separate the things that have been combined, he or she can use increasingly perfected markets to get one or all of these items from someone else. Either we multiply to create the unbundleable or the consumer will go ahead and do the hyphenation.

Let us use a simple example to explain what we mean. One of Kellogg's latest products is called Choco-Cornflakes. What you get is ordinary cornflakes with chocolate flavor. If the company had just used simple addition, it would have put one bag of cornflakes and one bag of chocolate powder in the cereal box. By pouring the ingredients into a bowl of milk we would get Choco-Cornflakes. Having done this once, it would be easy for us to unbundle the offering and get one box of ordinary cereal and milk chocolate from another supplier. So, Kellogg's uses multiplication. By covering every single cornflake with chocolate, the firm makes it much harder for the consumer to un-bundle the product (if you have a lot of time and patience just try it and go bananas). A weird example maybe, but the underlying logic applies to any business or activity. Successful hyphenation requires multiplication – unbundleability.

Winner takes all

Do you by chance remember Wally Masur? Didn't think so. In the early 1990s, Wally was one of the best tennis players in the world. He was in the top 50 and his career peaked in 1993 when he reached the semi-finals at the US Open, one of the four Grand Slam tournaments. Still, Mr Masur never ever got a contract to endorse either a tennis shoe or a racket.[75] In comparison with Andre Agassi and Pete Sampras, Wally Masur was not interesting or good enough for the Nikes and Adidas of the world to contact him. If you can get the best of the best, why settle for anything less? Almost, just isn't good enough. Sorry, Wally.

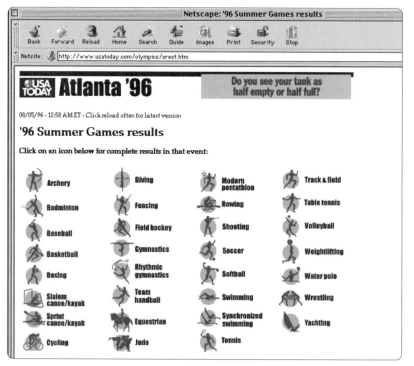

Had the Swedish athletes performed only 5 percent better they would have won more or less every medal on display

Our home country Sweden is a place covered with more snow and ice for a longer part of the year than anyone sane can really stand. Still, we left the 1998 Winter Olympics in Nagano, Japan, without a single gold medal. But, had the Swedish athletes performed only 5 percent better in speed skating, cross-country skiing, the downhill, etc. they would have won more or less every medal on display. Small differences but colossal consequences.

Entering a global excess economy marked by close to friction-free markets, there is a clear risk (or chance) that the winner will take all. In a borderless world, individuals or companies that are perceived as being only 1 percent better, or those that get a headstart and can use this initial advantage to gain even more reputation and market share, may kill all the others. Just look at Microsoft. Its operating system was perhaps not the best, but the firm managed to establish a world standard, got other software companies to write apps for their system and built in switching costs for all users. (Just imagine the extra costs of changing to a non-Windows-compatible operating system.) Microsoft smartly surfed the waves and, in effect, ended up with (close to) a global monopoly. And the company keeps on surfing the waves – adding on Microsoft Explorer free of charge to crush Netscape – at least until the US government sends out its Baywatch lawyers to close down the beach.

We see such developments all over the world. Why listen to the local bard or band when you can get a Madonna, Eagle-Eye Cherry or Pavarotti CD? Why use a local body builder in an action movie, when people are only interested in Sly Stallone, Arnie Schwarzenegger or Bruce Willis? Why watch a local soccer game when you can watch the best football team in Europe, Manchester United, playing Juventus on TV? Why use a second-rate architect to design your house, when you can get the best? Global stars capture all the attention and make ridiculous sums of money.

Ironically, the turbo market capitalism of our times comes with a built in bomb. In many cases, it will self-destruct. Maybe it won't happen within the next five seconds – reality isn't an episode of *Mission Impossible* – but strong forces eventually push international surplus competition toward global monopolies. We will not see the extreme consequences of this trend in all industries – one bar, one barber, etc. – but particularly when brains, the Net, and increasing returns come into play, potential worldwide monopolies await.

There are extreme economies of scale in most knowledge-intensive activities, at least if knowledge can be codified and frozen in atoms. The first copy of a CD-ROM, for instance, will cost enormous sums of money to develop and produce, but the next copy is almost free. Consequently, the incentives for capturing 100 percent of a global market are great, and the costs for doing so diminish dramatically the more customers the company can attract. The process accelerates still further if consumer value increases with the number of people who have access to or use what is offered. The Net is perfect for this kind of business as customers basically participate in the creation of value – prosumption. The more people who visit Yahoo, amazon.com, *et al.*, the better the service these companies can provide and the more people will come. This explains why so many Internet companies sacrifice short-term profits for growth. Mary Meeker, Internet analyst at Morgan Stanley, says, "On the Web, being No. 1 is awesome, No. 2 is OK, No. 3 is tough, No. 4 is the pits, No. 5 'Huh? Who?'."[76]

Global stars capture all the attention and make ridiculous sums of money.

Recipe-based competition

We are entering a world marked by techno-economic parity – dog eat dog days are here. In this surplus society, very few commodities, technologies, products, services, insights, knowledge areas or procedures that can be found in Berlin, Birmingham and Tokyo, Helsinki and Dallas are not also available to people in Singapore, Prague, Moscow, Mexico City and Manila. If this is

Competitiveness is all about recipes

really so, no person or firm can any longer base their sustainable competitive advantage solely on access to abundant resources.

Instead, as Stanford's Paul Romer puts it, the one with the best recipe will win. The individual, tribe, organization or region that excels in developing innovative concepts and ideas about how to combine and re-combine the ingredients will be most successful. We all need a recipe that is unique enough to capture the attention of oversupplied and demanding customers, a recipe that adds real value, a recipe that is difficult for the others to copy. And, in a winner takes all type of society, we must all realize that if we fail in developing the tastiest of recipes, this may very well be our Last Supper.

4

"Destroy to build"
MAO ZEDONG

FUNKY INC

Love them or loathe them, companies remain the powerhouses of the capitalist system. "Corporations are the dominant social institutions of our age," says Richard Pascale, author of *Managing on the Edge*.[1] Just think of a single fact: the 300 largest multinational companies control 25 percent of all the productive assets on earth.[2] A company such as Philip Morris has a larger annual turnover than New Zealand's GDP.[3] Half of world trade is handled by multinational companies.[4] Forget the Romans or the British Empire. These global firms are the new empires roaming and running the world.

What is impressive about these empires is that they are built around an empty legal entity. Corporations are legal frameworks. They are shells. A company or a business firm basically consists of four different things: *capital*, dollars, nickels and dimes; *machinery* and *buildings*, the dirty and expensive hardware; *people*, the problematic software; and a basic *idea*, the most elusive element of all.

While we salute the massive power wielded by corporations we know that they will look and behave differently tomorrow. In a global, real-time, brain-based and messy world, the inflexible structures of the past do not stand a chance. But, funky organizations do not merely adapt to these trends. They are not mirrors, reflecting changes in the environment. Funky organizations build mirrors – mirrors reflecting images that people have never seen before. They enable us to see what was once invisible – what was not. They reshape our perception of what is. Or, to paraphrase George Bernard Shaw's 1903 play, *Man and Superman*: the reasonable organization adapts itself to the world; the unreasonable one persists in trying to adapt the world to itself.

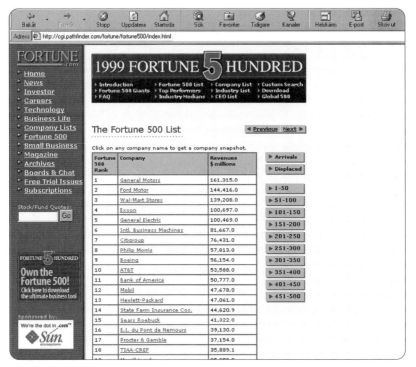

The 300 largest multinational companies control 25 percent of all the productive assets on earth

As a result, progress depends on the unreasonable organization. Ken Olsen, founder of Digital Equipment Corp., phrased it differently – but the sentiments are the same: "The best assumption to have is that any commonly held belief is wrong."[5] Success comes from shaping the future. Success is about creation, not adaptation.

Andy Warhol did it. Charlie Parker did it. Michael Dell did it. Muhammed Ali did it. They created something new, vibrant and original. They created what was not. Some people were predictably outraged and dismissed them as cranks. But, as Yossarian in Joseph Heller's novel *Catch-22* concludes, "Of course it's insane ... That's why it's the only sane thing to do." Sanity and sameness are overrated. Art will never be the same. Jazz will never be the same. The computer business will never be the same. Boxing will never be the same. Insight is like HIV. There are no remedies. Once you have it you cannot get rid of it. True entrepreneurs and entrepreneurial organizations offer us the opportunity to take a bite of an apple from the tree of knowledge. Then, there is no way back. Why else did God expel Adam and Eve from paradise?

Organizations come and go. They rise and fall. They change shape constantly. They leave the nations and regions in which they were born. They reorganize, realign, refocus. Nothing stays the same. But fear not, Funky Inc. is already here. Funky Inc. isn't like any other company. It is not a dull, old conglomerate. It is not a rigid bureaucracy. It is an organization that actually thrives on the changing circumstances and unpredictability of our times. Its difference – and its perpetual search for difference – is visible both in terms of its looks and how it operates. Funky Inc. is:

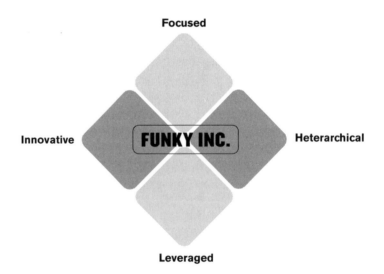

Funky Inc. is focused

Entering the age of abundance, we have to stop believing that organizations can master all things and situations. As long ago as 1776, the economist Adam Smith pointed out that as the size of a market increases so should the degree of specialization.[6] Two hundred years later there are no more geographical limits to push. We are there.

Stakeholders, inside and outside the firm, now have the power of choice. They all have access to international markets. None of them will accept middle-of-the-road models. The excess economy is ruthless. For the demanding customer, only the best will do, and no one can excel at everything. Global competition in an oversupplied world with increasingly perfected markets kills average product offerings and performers.

There are also internal factors that prevent us from spreading our resources too thinly. No matter how much digitization, globalization and deregulation we may experience, we are still human beings with limited cognitive capacity.[7] Our brains just don't have the bandwidth to handle excessive breadth. There is no way we can attend to everything with the same energy and emphasis.

Stakeholders, inside and outside the firm, now have the power of choice. They all have access to international markets.

Then there is the question of the internal climate of the organization. In non-focused firms, money is often reallocated from winners to losers, leaving people in the profitable businesses disappointed and demotivated. Likewise, there is a risk that the underperformers will doze off and rely on the others to save their necks yet again. Time is spent on political rather than productive matters. A sense of clarity and urgency is lacking.

In a society where money flows freely across borders, the shareholder will accept nothing less than continuous and fantastic value-creation. Increasingly perfected markets and total transparency prevent the pursuit of "unnatural" synergies. The management team of any diversified organization is basically saying that it is better than the market at balancing risk and creating value. But, actors in the market can now evaluate each business separately. If they come to the conclusion that the sum of the parts is actually greater than the present whole, they will step in and dismantle the company. Why should some overpaid president manage my investments? If I want a diversified portfolio, I will put it together on my own or turn to an expert on such matters.

As an effect of increasing customer, employer and shareholder pressure, more and more hierarchies are being engulfed by markets. Perfected markets hate inefficiencies so inefficiencies disappear. Inept organizations are dismembered or they die. So, funky organizations do not aspire to be everything for everyone. Instead, they try to become something for someone. This focus has three elements.

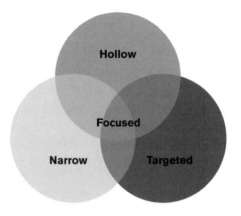

Narrow focus

Funky Inc. is narrow, focused on one or just a handful of core businesses. One of the reasons for the popularity of conglomerates, among theorists as well as practicing managers, was the idea of synergy. This was – and depressingly, still is – the ugly stepchild of corporate strategy. The management guru Igor Ansoff first proposed synergy in the 1960s.[8] It is a saddening thought that while the rest of the world enjoyed the overflowing excess of the Summer of Love, managers got down to synergy. Igor Ansoff was no Jimi Hendrix or Jim Morrison, but his message lives on. Managers fell in love with the potent simplicity of his concept. In their minds 2 + 2 really could equal 5. Managers had no need for hallucinogenics.

In retrospect, synergy cast a haze over rational managerial thought. This lingered for quite a while. Synergy gave managers an excuse to manage bigger and bigger companies. Indeed, during the mid-1980s, top management at Volvo developed the brilliant idea that there were synergies between beer, sports equipment, aspirin, hot dogs, cars, trucks, and buses. While there are certain synergies between beer and aspirin, they are difficult to exploit other than at an individual level.

Others have followed similarly irrational routes, proclaiming that owning a whisky distillery in Scotland will add value to the performance of the locomotive-making subsidiary in Nairobi. Next time you hear the word synergy, cock your guns. Often 2+2=3.5 instead of 5. Synergy is an expression of the managerial belief that it is much more fun to manage a large company than a small one. After all, you get to make speeches, meet kings and queens, smoke cigars and drink cognac, while presidents of small, excellent companies are left out in the cold – no matter how profitable they are. At a time of local and limited competition, this logic might just have worked – many Third World conglomerates are still successful in their protected home markets. In the kingdom of the blind, the one-eyed man could still be CEO. Today, it will not work. In the face of oversupplied international markets with total competition, we all have to realize that only the best is good enough. If you have stopped believing in Santa Claus, you may as well give up believing in synergies too.

The other classical argument for conglomerates was that of spreading risk – not placing all your eggs in one basket. But in a world characterized by genuine uncertainty and total unpredictability, we can no longer believe in minimizing risk. Indeed, we now need to embrace risk rather than try to eliminate it. Contemplating the fact that TetraPak, Swedish packaging giant, had bet its future on one product, former owner Hans Rausing once claimed, "We minimize risk by maximizing risk."

Put all this together and the message must be that the days of the large and diversified conglomerate are over. In an age of abundance, sharp is beautiful; being sharp and narrow is ravishingly beautiful. The antidote to mindless pursuit of synergies is to become intensely focused on those businesses where you clearly have a global competitive edge. Companies have to be turned from blunt instruments into sharpened precision tools.

Organizations are already honing themselves. How narrow a company is can be measured in terms of Standard Industry Codes (SICs), the number of different industries in which the firm is active. In the late 1970s, the average American firm scored a little more than four SIC, a few years back this measure was down to a little more than two.[9] Translation: the typical US company has lost some 50 percent of its body parts in less than 20 years. The excess economy is a pretty demanding weight watcher prescribing tough diet programs. The perfected market functions as a modern age Dr Frankenstein, cutting off and collecting spare body parts wherever and whosoever they may be.

Hollow focus

The second characteristic of focused Funky Inc. is that it is hollow. Focusing on only a few businesses just isn't enough. As strategy guru Gary Hamel sometimes puts it, you can take a fat man and cut off one of his legs, but that won't really make him any thinner. Every little process and activity in the firm must be exposed to the question: are we really world class? If not, outsource it. Buy it from someone else – someone who is better. Funky Inc. competes on the basis of its core competence and *competents*, the people who make competences happen.[10]

In an economy where you can buy most of what the typical company is doing just by searching the Internet or by flicking through the Yellow Pages, the "un-hollow" are doomed. In most large cities the Yellow Pages now covers 1600 rather than 160 pages and new websites with product offerings are added by the hour and by the minute. Surplus again. As noted earlier, globalization and digitization combined have dramatically changed the outcome of the classical fight between markets and hierarchies – make or buy. Over time, the odds change. Today, markets rule more than ever. What was logical and sound a few years back is now ludicrous and stupid. What makes sense today will probably not do so tomorrow. It's a never-ending story. Change, then change again.

Imagine that your company is built of Lego. Pick up a piece and ask yourself – are we the best company in the world at information systems – no that is Andersen Consulting or Cap Gemini – so let them take care of it. Are we the best company in the world at cleaning offices – no that is ISS – so let them take care of it. Are we the best company in the world at accounting – no that is Ernst & Young – so let them take care of that stuff. It is a simple principle. The logic is even simpler. Sooner or later, and in most cases sooner rather than later, all processes will be exposed to global competition.

The principle of aiming for top standards can be applied to all aspects of life. For instance, one of the authors admits that he is not the best chef in the world, so he often goes to restaurants. Nor is he the best window-cleaner in the world, so a window-cleaner visits his home every month. Unfortunately, he also has to admit that he is not the best lover in the world, so he and his wife have decided that once a week there is this guy who comes to their house and ... We're just kidding. They watch a lot of TV. They saw the woman in the commercial, changed their minds and bought her a Mercedes-Benz.[11]

Identifying core competences is navel-gazing. Look inside and discover yourself. Soul-searching. What are you really good at? What are you better than everyone else at doing? In what ways do these competences add value, and to which customers? How many of your employees share these competences? How difficult would it be for your competitors to copy them?[12] These are simple questions but the answers can reshape entire businesses.

Once organizations really start trying to identify their core competences, many of them realize that these are not always in

Atoms just aren't scarce enough so it is increasingly difficult to base competitiveness on access to them.

the areas they thought they would be in. American Airlines, for example, realized that its real strengths were tied to SABRE, the booking system, rather than operating airplanes. In 1995, SABRE alone accounted for 44 percent of the company's pre-tax profits.[13] Sears discovered that its critical skills were in the fields of logistics and branding, rather than in running department stores. GE, IBM, and Xerox are all experts in the area of consulting. Their products have become nothing more than byproducts, a sideshow to the main action. Again, we can see the shift from atoms to bits. Atoms just aren't scarce enough so it is increasingly difficult to base competitiveness on access to them.

Focusing on your core competences means sticking to what you excel at. A few years ago, if you drove a Toyota it was only 25 percent Toyota, whereas a GM car was 47 percent GM.[14] GM decided to add customer value and create a competitive edge by manufacturing its own car stereos. At Toyota, management argued that other companies such as Sony or Philips are much better at this so why bother – and then just how important is the car stereo when you buy a new car? We won't embarrass GM with a table depicting its well-managed, gradual decline over the last 20 years.

Do it well. Do it fantastically well. And then stop. Nike has struck gold by not applying its slogan.[15] Instead of just doing it – the company just doesn't do it. Funky Inc. brings in other people to do the rest. Many successful firms no longer make what they sell. Timberland, for instance, is a shoeless shoe company. Funky Inc. looks like the façades from an old Hollywood motion picture – nice on the outside, virtually empty on the inside, save for one thing: brains.

Look at the computer company Dell. It is a huge company that has come from absolutely nowhere. It is a huge company in terms of sales, but it does not have a single factory. There is no such place as a Dell factory. What founder Michael Dell realized was that, "IBM took $700-worth of parts, sold them to a dealer for $2000 who sold them for $3000. It was still $700-worth of parts."[16] By short-circuiting the market, by eliminating unnecessary actors who did not add any value to the customer, he created a business empire. Dell became an intelligent and flexible broker of parts, the professional procurement department of every single customer. "If this works for computers, it's going to work for automobiles, furniture, carpets, appliances, anything," says Larry Bossidy, CEO of Allied Signal, who recently invited Michael Dell to give a presentation to the management team of his organization.[17]

You can call this new firm virtual, hollow, a spider's web, outsourced, a shamrock, or whatever you like. The important thing is that if we don't slim down, our chances of surviving and thriving in an excess economy are just that – slim. Call it hollow, but don't call it empty.

An organization may hollow itself in a number of different ways. Quite often people only think about leaving more stuff to the suppliers – backward disintegration. But, hollowing out can also mean handing over activities to the customers – just think of IKEA. The typical Internet banks, for instance, enable us to pay our own bills – forward disintegration. Viewing the company as a collection of Lego pieces, it is basically up to each and every part of the organization to design its own role in contributing to the value of the whole. It used to be a question of adding stuff – integration. Now we focus on subtracting activities – disintegration. Funky Inc. may not incorporate an entire value chain, but it always has a position. In fact all companies have positions. It is just a question of what we buy and what we make. And by focusing on a few key value-adding processes and eliminating unnecessary actors, we make the rest of the value chain, as well as end-users, extremely dependent on us. And dependence equals dollars.

However, there is something beyond core competences. What is critical in the funky firm is perhaps not so much the core competences as the "core competents". These are the limited numbers of people at a company who actually embody the skills that make the products and services unique – Mr and Mrs Indispensable. These are the Mick Jagger and Keith Richards of the corporate world. And most of them are way too competent to be wasted in management positions. They are critical because (a) they are super-smart, and/or (b) they know who is smart, where these people are located and how to get them to cooperate.

These "walking monopolies" will only stay as long as the organization can offer them something they want. If that is no longer the case they will leave to set up their own one-person companies. Remember that Karl Marx was right. The workers currently own the most critical resources, the major assets of society. While competents personify prospective cores, it is our experience that competences, at least as popularly defined and used, often represent retrospective scores. Instead of looking into the future, many companies look into the past.

What is critical in the funky firm is perhaps not so much the core competences as the "core competents".

Nathan Myhrvold of Microsoft argues that we've got to understand that in a knowledge-based society, the difference between the average and the really good is no longer a factor of 1:2, as it used to be. No, it is a factor of 1:100, or even 1:1000.[18] His boss, Bill, sometimes says that if 20 people were to leave Microsoft, the company would risk bankruptcy. Hiroshi Yamauchi at Nintendo, the computer game company, echoes the same line of reasoning. He claims that an ordinary person cannot develop a really good game no matter how much he or she tries.[19] Or listen to what Sun Microsystems' CEO Scott McNealy has to say about fellow founder Bill Joy: "AT&T has Bell Labs, and we have Bill Joy. We get a lot more for our money."[20]

Core competents are omnipresent. In a recent study by the Corporate Leadership Council, a "computer" firm recognized 100 core competents out of 16,000 employees; a "software" company had 10 out of 11,000; and a "transportation" group deemed 20 of its 33,000 employees as really critical. In other words, the percentage of core competents varied between 0.6 percent and 0.06 percent. No wonder that, despite high unemployment rates, so many organizations speak of an ongoing talent war.

Targeted focus

The third and final element to Funky Inc.'s focus is that it is targeted. Funky Inc. targets tribes – core customers – and it doesn't matter what kind of tribe, where it's based or how large it is. What does matter is that they share a common vibe – values and attitudes.

Violent drug barons create tribes. Miguel Caballero is the Armani of the armored apparel world. His company sells customized and fashionable bullet-proof vests. It has targeted a specific tribe. Its home base is Columbia where demand is great.[21]

Pilgrims create tribes. Every year, 75,000 Chevrolet Suburban vans are sold in Saudi Arabia.[22] But why is this country such a huge market for the Suburban? The reason is that the pilgrims who visit Mecca are only allowed to enter the city in a vehicle with specific measurements. The only car that fits the specs happens to be the Chevrolet Suburban. In an unlikely "holy" alliance a US firm profits from aiding the Muslim tribe.

Leg fetishists create tribes. A while back, we came across a magazine called *Legshow*. It is a global magazine for people obsessed with naked legs and feet. A small market, one would have thought. Surely, foot fetishists cannot form a huge percentage of society. The reality is that the publishers of *Legshow* make more money in relation to its turnover than you would ever imagine. Why? It dominates a certain tribe. *Legshow* has developed a profitable niche. It does not have a foothold in the market, but has a very large boot covering all of the market – globally.

The message is that if you focus your energy on creating and then exploiting an extremely narrow niche you can make a lot of money. The tribe may consist of one-legged, homosexual dentists. It may be lawyers who race pigeons. But if you manage to capture these customers globally, you can make a lot of money. In an excess economy, we find riches in niches.

It is easier said than done. You have to get it right. You have to provide exactly the right offering for a clearly identified tribe and then deliver it repeatedly. There may only be 60 *Legshow* customers in Sweden, 55 in Norway, and 96,453 in France, but as we begin to conquer country after country it adds up to a lucrative business.

Forget about legs for a while. A friend of ours recently bought a new car and called all the major insurance companies in Scandinavia to check out what they could offer. Honest to a fault, he confessed to having a lengthy criminal record, drinking a bottle of vodka every day, and never going to bed without smoking pot. To his astonishment, he still hasn't been contacted by any of the companies.

The message is that if you focus your energy on creating and then exploiting an extremely narrow niche you can make a lot of money.

This is when we realized that we had stumbled upon the perfect business idea: an insurance company for alcoholics, junkies and criminals.

Of course, the trouble with such brilliantly simple entrepreneurial ideas is that there is often someone else who got there before you. But, surely not. Insurance for junkies and alcoholics? For the dull, unimaginative insurance industry we thought that these would be tribes too far. It is one thing to target 65-year-old retired middle managers with a pension and carefully amassed savings, another to insure the detritus of society. We were wrong.

Progressive Corp. does just that and it is such a good idea that it is now the sixth largest car insurance company in North America, and one of the most profitable.[23] Naturally, its strategic focus on this tribe is not the only critical success factor. The company has found the key to unlock this goofy niche by being extremely customized. Progressive is always open. Twenty-four-hour service is not just a slogan. When one of its customers crashes – and, given its clientele, this happens from time to time – Progressive rushes to the scene and tries to work things out with the other party. By doing so, it often manages to avoid bringing lawyers into the process. In the litigious US, this means cutting total process costs from an average of $9400 to $2100. As a consequence, Progressive can offer decent rates to junkie, former getaway drivers with drinking problems.

Such tidy and lucrative solutions exist in all industries. They may not always be made up of alcoholics, junkies, or criminals, but they do exist. We only have to develop a recipe that is tasty enough.

As you'd expect, the founder of Progressive, Peter Lewis, is far from conventional. His "friends" sometimes call him "a functioning pothead", "a frame or two off the ordinary radar-screen", and "a rock star without any musical ability".[24] Peter Lewis is more than 70 years old. He is a core competent. The company is so heavily dependent on him that a few years ago Wall Street analysts wanted to force him to get a physical examination. Peter Lewis didn't really fancy going to the doctors so he sent them a note instead. The note said:

"1 I feel fine.
 2 I swim a mile every day.
 3 I'm single, so I get laid a lot."

The first wave of funk killed those organizations that were not narrow enough. Conglomerates, where management could not convince the market that synergies were more real than UFOs, were chopped into pieces. The second wave of funk is now ripping process after process and activity after activity out of the bodies of un-hollow corporations. These organizations are forced to adapt or die. And in the not too distant future those companies not targeted on a specific tribe may well be the next victims of funk. Only the focused will flourish.

Funky Inc. is leveraged

The second crucial aspect of Funky Inc. is that it is leveraged. In recent years management and corporations have sought to solve the corporate puzzle through an obsession with minimization. Huge sprawling companies have sought to minimize bureaucracy, numbers of employees and to minimize time. Now, we need to maximize. Simply put, you cannot shrink to greatness. Downsizing easily becomes dumbsizing instead of rightsizing. Companies should not be neutron bombed. Or as Stanford's Jeffrey Pfeffer puts it, "Downsizing will only do one thing: make the organization smaller."[25] There is no way of creating new wealth by simply reducing costs and getting rid of people. Texas chainsaw massacre management does not result in revenue growth.

Once an organization has identified its basic businesses, the core capabilities and the target tribe, it needs to leverage its key resources. Funky Inc. needs to move on from corporate liposuction and anorexia to corporate bodybuilding – getting rid of the fat and letting the muscles grow.

In the machine age, leverage often meant real diversification – we needed different machines to make different products. But in a brain-based world, one and the same competence can be used to enter an array of industries, without being involved in the actual production of stuff as such. As noted earlier, the result is blur. The globally linked society forces firms to leverage competence in new ways and increased digitization enables and opens up the means by which this can happen. As with hollowing, leveraging is a three-stage process.

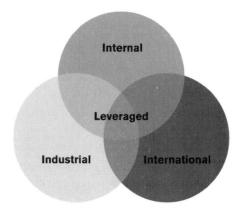

Internal leverage

The problem with most organizations is not that they know too little, but that they do not know what they know. Knowledge is dispersed without anyone having a clear picture of the total stock, how and where it flows, nor the location of specific capabilities.

To thrive, we must create a learning organization. This requires us to realize and acknowledge that we are not perfect. Unfortunately, this is often something which managers and companies are unwilling to contemplate. They should perhaps remember Arthur Koestler's definition of creativity as "a type of learning where the teacher and the pupil are located in the same individual".[26]

Building a learning organization is about increasing the rate of knowledge *transfer* and *transformation*. This starts with leveraging knowledge throughout the firm. We must move knowledge from individual levels to group and organizational levels. This sounds simple, but let us ask you three simple questions.

1 Are some of your colleagues better performers
   than others?
2 Would you like the others to become as good?
3 What is being done about it?

Learning does not happen automatically, it must be managed. And the speed of a company will be determined not by the fastest and smartest people but by the slowest and least skilled. Enabling learning is one of the key tasks for any leader. Leaders must ensure the continuous transfer of knowledge across organizational boundaries. The individual parts must be able to reflect the whole. In effect, Funky Inc. must work in a similar way to the human brain.[27]

Creating a learning organization is only part of the story. Customers do not pay companies – not even universities – for their learning abilities. They open their wallets for companies that can teach them something. So, in a real-time world we must decrease the time from insight to output. "An organization's ability to learn, and translate that learning into action rapidly is the ultimate competitive business advantage," says GE's Jack Welch.[28]

Unless the capabilities can be put to good use, they are virtually worthless. But creating such an organization is costly – IT investments, more travelling, co-location of key people and other measures do not come cheaply. The more important question, however, is whether you can afford not to invest in building a learning organization. Or as Johan Stael von Holstein, founder of the Web agency Icon Medialab, puts it, "If you think competence costs – try incompetence."

As a result, a critical task for any organization is to turn the core competents into core competences. The funky firm transforms human capital into structural capital – just as the Scandinavian insurance company Skandia is trying to do.[29] They collect the knowledge of the gold-collar workers and excellent teams. By building systems containing this competence, the firm provides **The manager becomes a kind of talk show host.** the others in the organization with an opportunity to learn and then use their new insights to help customers. Inevitably, this process calls for open communication and discussions throughout the entire company (and the external network). It may well be that the prime denominator of future competitive advantages will be related to which people are allowed to have what discussions about which topics with whom, when, and where.[30] The manager becomes a kind of talk show host. The question of whether one should try to be the Jerry Springer or the Oprah Winfrey of the firm, we leave to you. Funky Inc. is built around forums, virtual and real, where people can meet, rather than boxes and arrows that isolate them in unbreakable silos.

But leveraging is not only a question of transferring skills across levels and transforming competents into competence, it also concerns transforming knowledge into forms which allow the organization to more effectively profit from it. Just as with many materials, any type of knowledge basically comes in three different forms: gas, fluid and solid. Gas is what we have in our minds. Fluid knowledge comes about when we discuss things with others. And solid knowledge is the stuff that is embodied in customer offerings, routines and systems. In effect, a car, a PC, a software program, an ice-cream or whatever is in reality nothing more and nothing less than frozen creativity. We get an idea (gas); start discussing it with others (fluid); and finally develop a customer offering (solid).

The more solid the knowledge, the more money one can make. As we begin to freeze creativity, we also create opportunities for greater economies of scale. Remember the CD-ROM? The first copy is incredibly expensive, but then costs drop dramatically. Or take a consultant. Traveling around the world as a free agent he or she can probably make a pretty decent salary if loaded with fluid knowledge. But by writing a best-selling management book, or developing a management information system – freezing the knowledge – he or she can utilize the benefits of more or less costless reproduction.

The problem with frozen creativity is that it is easy for our competitors to pick up a copy, take it to pieces and copy it. The icier it gets, the easier imitation becomes. And no longer can we put our trust in patents. We must rely on our ability to develop processes that enable us to deep-freeze new pieces of knowledge faster than the others – decreasing the duration of the insight-output cycle. The alternative is to bundle our frozen knowledge with more fluid or gas-like stuff – to sell provices and serducts. Think about GE, Xerox, and IBM where the products are now little more than byproducts. The IT-experts Gartner Group predict that in 2003 services will represent 46 percent of IBM's revenues.[31] But the real route to enhanced competitiveness is to combine and constantly bundle and re-bundle these different forms of knowledge – hyphenation.

How we create and leverage the knowledge of the firm are critically important questions. But increasing internal leverage does not mean creating a department for learning or knowledge management. Many companies in the West are now repeating the mistakes they made when realizing that Japanese firms constantly beat them on quality. The answer then, as it seems to be now when knowledge is concerned, was to set up a department to handle the task. Quality was made into a big thing for a selected few, and we ended up with a bunch of quality engineers or managers running around trying to fix all the problems. Did it help? Not one bit. We must avoid making this mistake yet again. Instead, these responsibilities should be an integral part of everyone's job. Rather than knowledge management, the key to increasing internal leverage is knowledgeable management.

Industrial leverage

Leverage is not only internal. With a clear focus on their key capabilities, funky organizations also use their core competences and competents to enter new industries. But they do so without trying to control all processes internally.

Think back some 75 years. In the early twentieth century when Ford was founded, the company tried to control all inputs to the process. As a car manufacturer used metals, you needed mines. The tires were made of rubber, so you invested in a rubber plantation. Ford became a conglomerate. It got obsessed with controlling all input materials necessary to make the product, rather than thinking about how its key capabilities could be leveraged into other areas.

The new logic means sticking to your competence, but utilizing these skills in more than one industry. Today, we see at least three different types of industrial leverage.

First, there is *attitude-based* leverage. Having understood the needs of and targeted a specific tribe, the organization may then use the fit in attitude to supply this tribe with more stuff. But it needs to convey the same vibe. The rap and hip-hop group the Beastie Boys, for instance, not only offers its tribe CDs and concerts, but magazines, T-shirts, and a radio station as well. The group has its own company, Grand Royal, which is also a record company signing new artists. Similarly, rap star Puff Daddy and

British group Underworld offer their own lines of designer clothing. They follow the tribe.

Second, many firms engage in *brand-based* leverage. Marlboro does it. Coca-Cola does it. Disney does it as a publishing, retailing, and theme park operating company. Consider Richard Branson's Virgin, which is involved in everything from airlines and railways to clothing and cosmetics and from pensions to Internet services. The organization slavishly applies the core values of the brand when deciding whether or not to enter a new industry. At Virgin a new customer offering must be:[32]

... of the best quality;
... innovative;
... good value for money;
... challenging to the existing alternatives; and
... add a sense of fun or cheekiness.

Virgin's management says that as many as 90 percent of the projects it studies are, at least potentially, extremely profitable, but if a fit to these values cannot be found, they are rejected.[33] Branson and his colleagues understand that a brand is more than a name or a logo – it is a promise and a contract with each and every customer with whom you are dealing. And if people feel that the offering does not live up to what they expect from the brand, they may well decide to stop buying the other stuff as well.

Third, there are lots of cases of more purely *competence-based* leverage. Honda focuses on engines, but utilizes its knowledge to make cars, motorcycles, and so on. 3M is an expert on adhesives. The Japanese company KAO is a major player in the branded packaged goods industry – diapers, shampoos, lotions, etc. A couple of years ago it was also one of the largest producers of floppy disks. Lotions and floppy disks? Well, if you believe that you are an expert in minimizing friction, maybe the logic isn't that strange. Or look at AT&T, which considers itself an excellent processor of transactions. It has a great brand and customer relationships characterized by permanence and trust. Put all this together and the company's move into the credit card business can be understood.

International leverage

No surprises, leverage needs also to be international. Funky Inc. is a global corporation. But global does not necessarily mean big. Midget multinationals – like *Legshow* – are already all around us. The next time you go to the dentist, ask if you can keep the slurp, the disposable saliva sucker. Take a look at it. There is a 50 percent chance that it comes from a division within the Swedish company Bergman & Beving. This unit holds a 50 percent global market share in the slurp industry. How many employees does it have? It has 85. If you are one of 85 people at a company with a 50 percent worldwide market share, you can really feel that you work in an international organization. Do all 416,000 employees at Siemens feel that way?

While globalization is here, it is often not readily recognized in the organization of firms. Although most companies *access* global markets through exports, and many have their *assets* internationally dispersed in the form of foreign subsidiaries, few have managed to build global *administrative* structures and systems.

We also see clear differences across geography. To the typical US multinational, foreign usually equals marginal. Well-known international companies such as Microsoft and Intel still generate more than 70 percent of their profits at home.[34] At many US firms, non-US business is still relegated to a box in the organizational chart called ROW (Rest of the World). At the traditional Japanese multinational, foreign equals different. Critical decisions are mostly made in Japan, by the Japanese.

But for many European multinationals, and particularly those from small countries such as Sweden, Finland, Holland, and Switzerland, foreign has always equaled "most of it". Early on, these companies had to come up with ways and solutions to tackle global challenges. The result is usually that the role of headquarters is not as pronounced. Percy Barnevik has described ABB's HQ as the place where the mail arrives before important letters are faxed to wherever he may be. These companies have many global centers of different kinds dispersed throughout the world.

HQ is the place where the mail arrives before important letters are faxed

So if you want to learn more about managing across borders look to European firms such as Philips, Electrolux, Nokia, Heineken, Unilever, TetraPak and Nestlé, rather than Chrysler or Mitsubishi.

And then there is the fourth and most important stage of globalization – *attitudes*. No company we have ever come across is truly global in attitude. Home-country standards are often applied relatively uniformly. Key persons usually come from the same country. Products are mostly developed at home with the requirements of the local market in mind. The typical multinational is still parochial and ethnocentric.[35] Foreigners are often regarded as strange. Or, as the Dutch expert on cross-cultural management Fons Trompenaars puts it, "Understanding culture still seems like a luxury item to most managers."[36] Letting one of these managers loose in another culture is like inviting an elephant to dance in a china store.

Yet, only when we have become truly global in attitude can we reap all the other benefits of funkiness. To succeed, we need to move from conflict to reconciliation.[37] We're not saying that it is easy to work in a global organization. Differences in culture and languages and large geographical distances provide demanding challenges. There will be disagreements and misunderstandings aplenty. A few years ago a successful European MNC we worked with was given two prestigious awards for promoting equality between the sexes. Before being presented with the awards, the CEO wanted to know exactly how equal the company was, in case someone asked. So, he sent a fax to all the subsidiaries asking for a report on the composition of the top management team broken down by sex. After two hours he received the first response. It was from the Finnish subsidiary: "Dear Mr President, we have no one in the top management team broken down by sex. However, we have one alcoholic." Globalization may be seen by many as a necessary evil, but that does not make it less essential.

Funky Inc. is innovative

Funky Inc. is extremely innovative. In a real-time, globally linked surplus society it is just a matter of a few weeks, days or even hours before our friends from Bangalore, New York, Kuala Lumpur, Paris, Gdansk, Tokyo, Seoul, London or Santiago come here to copy our recipes. To remain unique, we must constantly sharpen our competitive edge. Alan F. Shugart, Chairman of disk drive giant Seagate Technology Inc., goes as far to say that, "Sometimes I think we'll see the day when you introduce a product in the morning and announce its end of life at the end of the day."[38] And IT guru Kevin Kelly says, "Wealth flows directly from innovation ... not optimization ... wealth is not gained by perfecting the known."[39]

By innovation we do not mean a dedicated department, a carefully fenced off group of boffins. We mean total innovation – a frame of mind that applies to everyone at the company, everything, everywhere, and that goes on non-stop. It turns the company into an idea and dream factory that competes on imagination, inspiration, ingenuity, and initiative.

Total innovation – a frame of mind that applies to everyone at the company, everything, everywhere, and that goes on non-stop.

If you think we are getting overexcited, think of an ordinary company selling some pretty dull products. Think of Rubbermaid that has been repeatedly selected as America's most admired corporation by *Fortune* magazine. This firm thrives on developing and producing plastic products such as buckets, dish brushes, and wastepaper baskets. To an uninspiring roster of products, Rubbermaid brings total innovation, imaginative zeal that converts the banal into something different and exciting. We draw the line at calling a bucket a sexy product.

Innovation permeates Rubbermaid.[40] Some time ago the management team visited the British Museum in London. They left the building with a bunch of new ideas for kitchen products. Apparently, the ancient Egyptians knew things we have forgotten. Rubbermaid pillaged the ancient past with pride and considerable gusto. If Rubbermaid can do it, so can you. Innovation is rewarded in every industry.

Innovation is not only a matter of technology – nuts and bolts. In fact, technology is often only a small part of it. Innovation concerns every little aspect of how an organization operates – administrative innovations, marketing innovations, financial innovations, design innovations, HRM innovations and service concept innovations. Going for total innovation, therefore, requires rethinking every little aspect of how we operate. This means reinventing strategy, increasing speed and thriving on smartness. But above all, total innovation requires ignoring *and* listening to the customers, as well as promoting internal heterogeneity *and* homogeneity – moving from a world of focusing on either or to one of achieving both, simultaneously. We are not talking about striking a balance – Funky Inc. combines extremes rather than settling for average solutions.

Innovate through reinventing strategy

In a world where technology, institutions and values are in a state of turmoil, innovation is about rethinking what we are doing and about reinventing our industry. The US company Taco Bell, part of Pepsi Co., sells "tex-mex" junk food. At one time, the company firmly believed that it was a player in the fast food industry, and that the key to success was to increase market share, particularly in relation to other tex-mex restaurants. Reviewing the strategy, management realized that Taco Bell was really in the business of feeding people.[41] The more challenging goal was to go for an increased share of stomach. In one second, the size of the market exploded from $70 billion to $550 billion. In five years, sales more than doubled. How? Well, if you are in the business of feeding people you better go out looking for the customers, rather than just expecting them to find you. So, Taco Bell set up small, often portable restaurants at schools, hospitals, train stations, airports, libraries and other such places.

During the last few years, we have seen companies such as Dell, amazon.com, Nike, and Starbucks doing the same thing. They change the rules of the game. The uniqueness of these firms often rests with the soft and intangible aspects of their customer offerings rather than technology. Nike shifted its focus from being a shoe company to being a sports company. And then it shifted the focus from sports products as such to sporting performance and the superstars of sports. While most people don't talk about the characteristics of a particular basketball shoe or a golf putter, many are willing to dissect the performances of Michael Jordan or Tiger Woods from every angle.

Howard Schultz, "the espresso evangelist", and Starbucks took on the Herculean task of educating the American consumer about the fine coffees of the world. Contrary to what many would have expected, the company turned out anything but a modern age Sisyphus. The main advertising instruments were the local coffee shops where so called baristas (bartenders) were trying to promote a lifestyle. And entering alliances with Barnes & Noble, Costco, United Airlines and others expanded this network.

There is nothing new about strategic innovation. In 1920, Ford had a 60 percent market share in the US automotive industry. It churned out one new, shiny black Model T per minute. General Motors had to settle for a paltry 12 percent of the market. Then, the legendary GM chief Alfred P. Sloan entered the stage. He reorganized the company into a multidivisional firm.[42] The new strategic objective was a car "for every purse and every purpose".[43] Three out of eight existing models were killed, and the remaining brands (Chevrolet, Oldsmobile, Pontiac, Buick and Cadillac) were each targeted at a particular segment of the market – and they came in more than one color. Henry Ford had to close down his Dearborn factory for a year.

Innovate through speed

Not only does a larger geographical market necessitate a sharper focus, it also decreases the time available to exploit our capabilities.

In a real-time society, getting to the future faster is obviously important. Funky Inc. operates in a world in which things are moving at a pace never before witnessed. No wonder that Gordon Forward, CEO of Chaparral Steel, concludes that, "To stand still is to fall behind."[44] Once we have a clear focus on our core competences, we need to act at the speed of light.

Traditionally, many European companies have been successful in what is usually referred to as mature industries. But, how can we then explain that a company like ABB generates half of its revenues from products introduced during the last three years? After you have erased the word synergy, please erase the word mature from your vocabulary and replace it with tired. We should no longer talk about mature industries or markets, but tired ones. Tired industries and markets are waiting for someone to do something revolutionary, radical, and interesting. If we are entering a real-time economy, a remote control reality, people will zap to another company the instant they find that you are old, boring, and out of date.

Speed rules and speed freaks

Boeing: In a matter of a couple of years, Boeing has managed to reduce the time it takes to build a 747 or 767 by approximately 50 percent to some 8 months.

Microsoft: Windows 95 was launched across the globe in one day.

McDonalds: The food chain establishes three new restaurants per day, every week, every month, year round, all over the world. And, at least a few years back, approximately 1 out of 15 Americans have their first job flipping Big Macs.

Innovate through smartness

Working faster is of course not a question of trying harder – just try doing the wrong things twice as fast – it is a matter of working smarter. Even though the new economy comes without speed limits, creativity can not be forced upon people. To be creative we need slack.[45] We need resources and time. We need time to sit down and reflect. We need time alone. We need time to play around. We need time to experiment. We need time to have casual conversations with others. In Japan, people sometimes refer to "nommunication", rather than communication. Nommu is Japanese for drinking – and for once we are not talking about Coke. The time spent together in a bar after office hours can be critical to the development of new ideas. A lot of venturing, mingling, socializing and relationship-building in Silicon Valley is done in bars. So if thinking is working, put your feet back on the table, then leave the office and have a drink with your colleagues. Cut yourself some slack.

In a knowledge-based society, brains will always beat brawn. We all know that. But, just how much of a company's intellectual capital is really used? If your organization is normal, and by God we hope it's not, the answers usually range from 5 to 15 percent. What would happen

No one can have a monopoly on creativity – not even Microsoft.

if a plant manager utilized only 5 to 15 percent of existing manufacturing capacity? This person would be replaced in months or even weeks. This is apparently not the case when knowledge is concerned. The company's most critical asset is massively underutilized. Little wonder that people usually seem a bit embarrassed when this subject comes up – but they do tend to comply. Maybe 15 percent isn't that bad after all? The only possible explanation is that somewhere along the line someone tricked us. They tricked us into believing that employment in reality only means "competence castration". As soon as we enter our office, the factory floor, or whatever, only 15 percent of our body is supposed to be present – let's hope it's the upper 15 percent.

We need whole persons – head and heart, body and soul. As it stands today, many organizations do not use knowledge – they abuse it. Something can be done and must be done. Remember what creativity expert John Kao says, "Creativity is not like the weather – you can do something about it."[46] And no one can have a monopoly on creativity – not even a momentary one – not even Microsoft.

Ignoring and listening to customers

Contrary to popular belief, getting to know customer requirements is not very difficult. Let us tell you what all customers want. Any customer, in any industry, in any market wants stuff that is both cheaper and better, and they want it yesterday. Organizations may spend millions of dollars every year getting McKinsey, Boston Consulting Group or A.T. Kearney to help them answer this question. But the simple truth is that the typical customer will always ask for improvements within the present frame.

Radical innovation in a discontinuous world means forgetting about forecasting and listening to marketing studies. Of course, history is littered with people who ignored customers and paid the price. Still, listening to the wrong customers, or listening without thinking, can be real killers as well.

Do you remember McLean, the low-fat hamburger from McDonald's? The product was introduced in response to the increased health-consciousness of the American consumer. The marketing tests revealed that it tasted almost as good as a Big Mac, but then no one ordered it. What did the company forget? Well, most people who enter a McDonald's restaurant are not health fanatics. The health-conscious eat elsewhere. The average McDonald's consumer is more interested in McLard than McLean.

The reality is that we use and enjoy products that we wouldn't have wanted if they had been proposed to us at the very start of their development. A fax? If I am in a hurry I will use the phone, otherwise I will send a letter. A VCR? If it's on TV I want to watch it live, and if it's a movie I want to go to the theater. CNN? More news, and in English? No thanks. Yet, we all know what happened. We cannot expect the customer to think the unthinkable. That is our task. The responsibility for innovation always rests with the supplier. We must have the gifts and guts to imagine and work wonders. All this implies risk – total risk – and, at the end of the day, personal risk.

Read our lips. You cannot expect the customer to think the unthinkable. You may well think of yourself as a demanding and sophisticated customer. You may well be right. But would you have imagined that there could be a market for a tiny electrical chicken which requires regular feeding, nurturing and entertainment otherwise it dies? Yet, the Tamagotchi – the tiny pet from cyberspace – was one of the great success stories of 1997.

Gallery visitors did not tell Picasso to invent cubism. Jazz fanatics did not suggest that Miles Davies should work with hip-hoppers. Moviegoers did not propose to Lars von Trier, the Danish film director, that he make *Breaking the Waves*. And customers sure as hell did not come up with the idea for CDNow or amazon.com. If you want to do something really interesting and revolutionary, learn to ignore your customers. Most customers function as rearview mirrors. They are extremely conservative and boring, lack imagination, and don't know their own minds. If customers are constantly beating you to new ideas, hire them or get another job.

Gallery visitors did not tell Picasso to invent cubism.

Does technology-push really work? Just look at the US biotech company Amgen. It has been among the top performers on the *Fortune 1000* in terms of profitability for the last ten years. The business concept of Amgen is to take brilliant science and find a use for it. It may well be that if customers don't like your solutions, they have the wrong problems. Unfortunately, in an age of abundance where the customers are in charge of the remote control, this is more problematic for you than for them.

If you are really innovative, you are also in a position to fire some of your customers. The typical company loses money on at least 50 percent of its customers. Trouble is, most companies do not have a clue about who these customers are. Clearly, the risks associated with voluntarily or involuntarily firing the wrong customers are immense. For Ford a 1 percent increase in customer loyalty is worth approximately $100 million per year in profits.[47] When an unhappy customer walks out the door, how much money does your organization lose if he or she decides never to come back? It could be $500, $5000, perhaps even $50,000.

Paradoxically, Funky Inc. must also be extremely customized. We have to choose. Sometimes we must ignore the customer and do something radical and revolutionary, and in certain cases we must look upon the customer as a part of the firm and include them in value-creation processes. In the age of the demanding customer, it is no longer enough to produce slides and slogans saying that the customer is king.

Customize, then do it some more. 3M's Post-it notes now come in 18 colors, 27 sizes, 56 shapes and 20 fragrances. All in all, more than half a million combinations are available.[48] The modularized trucks of SCANIA allow you to build your personal truck – cafeteria style. Or why not build your own doll? Barbie now comes complete with 15,000 combinations. The management gurus were right. Mass customization is child's play. Change the outfit, the eyes, the color, the hairdo, the clothes, the name – but don't even think about the legs. All for $40 (double the usual price).[49] To get the customized doll, you need to fill out a questionnaire. Anne Parducci, VP of Barbie's owner Mattel, claims that the aim is to "build a database of children's names, to develop a one-to-one relationship with these girls".[50] George Orwell eat your heart out, 1984 is here (a little late perhaps). And what do you think is valuable at Mattel – hundreds of kilos of doll-atoms or the brand and the database? Bits rule.

In a fragmenting world, niches are becoming ever smaller. Increasing individualization combined with changes in technologies and values mean that micro markets have overtaken mass markets. The next step is one-to-one manufacturing, one-to-one marketing, one-to-one everything, one customer–one solution. It is happening in industry after industry. We are entering a one-to-one society.[51]

Look at yourself in the mirror and staring back at you is the average size of a market segment in a surplus society. The new logic of the demanding customer is really simple. It is up to you to satisfy me, and I am not like you, you, or you.

Customization can occur in all aspects of the customer offering; customized products, customized prices, customized opening hours, customized promotion, etc. Total customization. Tele-operators and utility companies let us design our own profiles for pricing and paying bills. MTV targets programming and commercials for different regions in Europe.

The recent developments in production equipment open up many new opportunities. We can move from mass production to flexible production and now mass customization. With fewer tools we can produce more and better-quality models.

Customization is also about your share of time. When and for how long are you prepared to do business with your clients? In an age of abundance, the customer decides when you can do business with him or her, not the opposite. Your only chance of survival is to move closer toward becoming a true 24-hour company – like Progressive Corp.

In addition, in some situations certain customers are your best consultants (and, always, the cheapest). The modern manager has one great advantage. Customers and employees have never been as smart as they are right now. The sensible executive treats them as assets, not assholes. A natural solution is to move power close to those people directly involved with the customers on a daily basis. Those engaged in the moment of truth activities, as former Scandinavian Airline Systems President Jan Carlzon put it, must be given the means to master the situation.[52]

"Anything you can digitize, you can customize," says Joseph Pine, author of *Mass Customization.*[53] "Everything that can be digital will be," claims New York-based digital change agent Razorfish.[54] So more or less everything is being customized. Do you have a pair of Levi's jeans? Do they fit perfectly? If the answer to the second question is negative, don't worry. Contact Custom Clothing Technology over the Internet. This company has a strategic alliance with Levi's. Just type in your measurements and two weeks later you will receive a pair of customized Levi's 505, or whatever. Extra cost – 10 dollars.[55]

You may not care that much for customized jeans. Each funky firm is not for everyone. We are talking super-specialization and ferocious focusing. And some will pay for it – though customization is not necessarily more expensive. Car rental company Hertz discovered that by doing only what each customer actually required, its Gold service was in fact less expensive to provide than its Standard service.[56]

Combining heterogeneity and homogeneity

Making radical changes possible calls for a much more personalized company. Oscar Wilde was right when he noted that, "Consistency is the last refuge of the unimaginative." Funky Inc. thrives on variation, difference, and diversity. Funky Inc. welcomes people who are prepared to challenge the status quo, and to break with existing norms and regulations. Funky Inc. refuses to take part in the look-alike game any more.

Quite often people talk favorably about diversity as it supposedly promotes a better atmosphere and equality. Though arguments alluding to the "fun and fair" consequences of increased variation may seem nice and laudable, this is not the stuff that convinces the typical manager to change the mix of people at the company. Instead, let us give you three solid economic reasons for the profitability of heterogeneity.

1 Because $C=D^2$, where C stands for creativity and D for diversity.[57] Lack of diversity often results in groupthink and intellectual constipation.[58] We all know what the others think, so what's the use in talking to them. From the point of view of innovation, opposites attract. Novelty is the result of constructive misfits and tension. Cacophony Inc. replaces calamity with creativity.

2 More diversity generally decreases the average performance of a system but it also increases the standard deviation. The

problem for Consistency Inc. is that in a world where the winner takes all, we do not compete on averages – we compete on exceptions. A firm with a lower average may well slaughter a rival with a higher average if the latter organization lacks unique ideas that totally deviate from the norm.

3 To ensure success, the complexity of our environment must be reflected in the composition of the firm. Most academics refer to this as the Law of Requisite Variety.[59] In practice, this means that when suppliers are from outside the home country of the organization this must be reflected in the make-up of the organization. If many of our customers are immigrants, this too must be reflected. If we deal with really young or old people this must be reflected. If we increasingly do business with women, this must be reflected.

Yet, most of us live and work in organizations built by and for 5 percent of the population – middle-aged white males. Management guru Tom Peters recently noted that women make some 65 percent of all car-buying decisions in the US. Why then are merely 7 percent of all car salespeople women?[60] Why do men design more or less all cars? Why do only men manage car companies? Again, this is not only a question of equality, it is a question of quality of decisions and customer offerings. It is a question of dollars, nickels and dimes. Case closed.

Unfortunately, many firms are so inbred that you sometimes expect the next person to walk through the door with an oversized head, red curly hair, and an extra eye in the middle of their forehead. Some organizations are like the Amish people. All people look the same and think that they can freeze time. Don't expect too much innovation at companies where 90 percent of the employees are the same gender, about the same age, have a similar educational background, dress the same way, and all play golf. Even if they go on annual strategy conferences to the Mediterranean or the Alps to be really creative, wild, and crazy, don't expect a great deal. A company with a board filled with white, male, 55-year-old Finns is unlikely to come up with an idea that is even slightly appealing to a young, colored, female,

Your new CEO?

lesbian, non-Scandinavian Muslim. Are the men on the board going to recruit Muslim lesbians? Of course not.

Perhaps the guy in the picture should be the next CEO of your company. Maybe he holds the knowledge that could make you unique in the twenty-first century. But, would you, under any circumstances, hire this person? And, more to the point, would this individual, under any circumstances, apply for a position with your company? The man in the picture is Virgin-owner Richard Branson.

What if you are continually turning down applications from Richard Branson types. Or even worse, maybe these guys have stopped sending their CVs to you because they know that you care about how people look, dress, the color of their skin, and so on.

We are not suggesting that you should start recruiting all the cross-dressers in the world, but simply that you have to be prepared for the consequences of developing a brain-based firm. And, allowing people to be themselves and to look as they want appears a fundamental starting point.

The competitive reality is that organizations that are bogged down in issues of race, gender, age, sexual preferences, look and so on, will slip deeper down in the mire. They will encounter serious problems when competition moves softwhere. Intelligence is normally distributed. It is not the preserve of white, 45-year-old males.

As Michael McNeal, Director of Corporate Employment at Cisco Systems, points out: "If you want to find great people you've got to look in unusual places."[61] Recruiting only from Harvard Business School or INSEAD in France, will result in a pretty homogeneous crowd. Instead, Cisco tries to find people at the Boston Marathon and the Mountain View International Microbrewery Festival.

Admittedly, an entire company of Richard Branson or Peter Lewis types would be quite difficult to manage. We are not saying that you should move from hierarchy to anarchy. Instead, we are simply suggesting that sharing a number of things will be helpful. What can you share? The choice is endless. How about shared ownership, rewards, identity, culture, language, knowledge and attitudes.

Kodak, Amgen, Cisco, Merck, General Mills and Procter & Gamble all have one thing in common; they offer stock options for all employees.[62] Marx meets the Wild Capitalist West. Shared ownership is increasing everywhere. At GE more than 20,000 employees are currently given stock options, as compared to merely 200 during the 1980s.[63] In 1996, the Bean Stock program at Starbucks coffee shops allowed employees who joined the firm in 1991 to cash in options for $50,000.[64] Fat bonuses are no longer necessarily the privilege of a select few. Power to the people. Remember that most software companies were incorporated to share ownership and wealth, not to raise capital. And we ain't seen nothin' yet.

Funky Inc. is neither homogeneous nor heterogeneous; it is *both*. Successful companies will evolve into organizational tribes – biographical organizational tribes.[65] And in a tribe people get the energy from one another. The Zulus have a word for it: "ubuntu" (short for unmunta ngumuntu nagabuntu). This can be translated, a person is a person because of other persons. Or as C. G. Jung put it, "I need we to be fully I."[66]

Let us ask you a personal question. Do you regularly visit lesbian clubs? Let's be honest now. Well, if you do, as a man you are struck by a number of things. No. 1 – there are a lot of women

Organizational tribes

in there. No. 2 – they're all so different – some are old, others young, some nurses, others business managers, students, doctors, everything that you could ever think of. The only thing these people have in common is their sexual orientation. By keeping one thing constant we allow for variation in all other dimensions.

At McKinsey and several other consulting firms, all the employees have at least one thing in common. They are insecure overachievers. This is a way of keeping people together and assuring some continuity in an otherwise discontinuous world. At Quad Graphics blood or marriage relates more than 50 percent of the 8500 or so employees.[67] Once, someone even said that the Mafia gets more resignations than a company such as 3M with its extremely strong culture.[68] Have you thought of, identified and worked with the lowest common denominator of your organization?

And just how do you get people to share your values? Short answer: find those who already do. Look at hell's angels or Greenpeace. "We hire attitudes," says Herb Kelleher of SouthWest Airlines.[69] The logic is that you can make positive people into good pilots, but turning great pilots with attitude problems into charming servers of customers is close to impossible. Funky Inc. recruits people with the right attitude, then it trains them in skills – not the reverse.[70] We can no longer bring in smart people and then brainwash them at training camps. Ideally, of course we try to attract people who are smart *and* share our values. But, if you are forced to choose, go for attitude. Lenin was right again. Find the revolutionaries. Do not try to change people.

The tribe is not necessarily restricted to the legal boundaries of the firm. Look at Harley-Davidson.[71] By inviting the consumer tribe it has targeted to join the organizational tribe, the firm has dramatically extended its community. It uses parties to initiate new members. Storytelling around the camp fire keeps the messages moving throughout the tribe. Closing ceremonies and continuous reinforcement are also part of the deal. What Harley-Davidson and other Funky Incs. have realized is that a tribe targeting another tribe does not merely have to produce value – the customers also want values.

Funky Inc. is heterarchical

A Greek called Dionysius the Aeropagite introduced the concept of hierarchy some 1500 years ago.[72] The word literally means "to rule through the sacred". Now, Dionysius was not the mythological wine lover. He was scholastic rather than alcoholic, interested in God and the Devil, in heaven and hell. Somehow, Dionysius figured out that heaven is (was?) hierarchically organized. Not only that, he also argued that this celestial structure had exactly nine levels with God as the CEO, the archangels making up the top management team, and Jesus Christ in a staff position to the right of God. If you fear that you may not end up in this place, do not worry. According to the Aeropagite, hell is also hierarchically organized – with nine layers. One might suspect that the entire structure is turned upside down, however, with purgatory as the prime motivator to "climb" the ladder.

Hierarchy builds on three key assumptions: your environment is *stable*, your processes are *predictable*, and your output is *given*. You know where you are, what you do, and what will happen – the same competitors, customers, suppliers, technologies and product offerings – year in and year out. As long as this holds true, it is utterly stupid to organize in any other way. However, we seriously doubt that you would use any of those three words to describe your reality. And in a surplus society, an economy moving forward at turbo speed, and in companies heavily reliant on brainpower, traditional hierarchies will get constant nervous breakdowns.

Hierarchy holds other negative consequences. Jack Welch of GE expresses it bluntly when he argues that hierarchy is an organization with its face toward the CEO and its ass toward the customer. Is Welch right? Pleasing the boss sometimes seems more important than serving the consumer. Hierarchy is usually easier for us, but is it better for the customer?

As hierarchy assumes that the sources underlying competitive advantage are given and eternal, the organizational challenge is to find a structure that will be an efficient exploiter of this specific combination of knowledge. So, we developed organizational structures that excelled in spitting out yet another standardized customer offering. But, in an age of abundance with total global competition, overcapacity in more and more industries, as well as increasingly powerful customers, we need to be different. We need innovation and renewal of our recipe. We need structures that support experimentation and the creation of novelty.

Hierarchy is an organization with its face toward the CEO and its ass toward the customer.

Funky Inc. applies organizational solutions capable of combining and recombining knowledge across any type of border at the speed of light. And hierarchy simply is not for hyphenation and combination, it is for separation and division. So forget organizational pyramids with the CEO sitting atop them. Who wants to work in pyramids, the greatest tombs ever created by man? Playgrounds must gradually replace the pyramids.

The funky model

The traditional hierarchical firm won't be a problem in the twenty-first century – it won't be around. The new organization will be heterarchical – containing many hierarchies of different kinds.[73]

In reality, all firms have three overlapping systems of positions, processes, and professions.[74] The positional structure is a contact book with addresses and numbers. The professional structure tells you something about the skills of people, and the process structure shows you what is actually going on. Everyone can be included in all of these categories, but in different places. The positional structures are manifested in our organizational charts. The process structures are represented by boundary-spanning activities and projects. The professional structures are a lot more messy and dependent on the skills of individuals placed all over the landscape of the firm, and increasingly also outside the legal boundaries of the company.

Historically, we have made the mistake of only recognizing the positional structure. Senior executives managed these structures, controlled all-important processes and projects, and their professional knowledge was regarded as omnipotent. Many companies still make this mistake. The typical boss, no matter what type of organization or formal position in the hierarchy, is obsessed with knowing and controlling everything. The basic assumption has been that as people are stupid, they can only handle really simple jobs so we better have super-complex organizational structures.

Today, we need to transform complexity into simplicity. Jack Welch goes as far as to call bureaucracy the Dracula of organizational design. No matter how much we fight it, bureaucracy always comes back to haunt us. So we have to keep putting stakes through its heart.

In the face of an increasingly complex knowledge landscape we have to strengthen the power of the professional and process structures. Firms need stronger project leaders as well as intellectual champions with sufficient organizational clout. But neither of these structures should dominate totally. If action drives the entire system the result is ad-hocracy and, if we let knowledge be the single organizing principle, the resulting structure is a meritocracy.

Total domination by one of the principles leads to bureau-*crazy*, ad-ho*crazy* and merito*crazy*, rather than anything else. All three aspects of the modern firm need to exist simultaneously – in our minds. And the latter point is critically important. The funky model is not a three-dimensional matrix. We will not solve problems by simply rearranging the boxes and arrows. It is a frame of mind, a philosophy. And we are not talking about a topless organization. The alternative to hierarchy is not *no-archy*. There is still a critical role for management to play. But they are no longer the only actors or stars.

The question must be whether or not we can see any companies successfully applying the funky model? Two of our colleagues recently studied the Danish hearing-aid company

Spaghetti organization

Oticon.[75] With some $100 million in annual sales, about 1000 employees and more than 90 percent of sales outside its home country, Oticon uses a "spaghetti organization". Just like in a boiling pot of spaghetti there is apparent disorder and chaos, but you can easily pull out a single strand of spaghetti and follow it from beginning to end. Every person in the firm belongs to a pool of resources. Any individual is tied to a project, a specialty profession, and to a people dimension. You are someone. You do something. You know something. Projects constitute the *modus operandi* at Oticon. At any given time there are some 90 projects. Specialty professions represent the functional organization where distinctive skills and expertise are developed. The people dimension refers to personal development. Rather than selecting people for fixed positions, Oticon tries to fit jobs to people. Successful? The firm will soon have been spaghetti managing for ten years, and is one of the most profitable companies in its industry.

Seven features of the funky firm

So how will Funky Inc. work? Well, let us provide you with seven principles for organizing the firm. Some you will recognize, but the real trick is getting them all to work together in harmony.

◼ Smaller

Throughout the twentieth century the predominant corporate myth was that big was good. From Henry Ford to Michael Eisner, Alfred P. Sloan to Jack Welch, size has been considered all-important. Bravado, of a peculiarly male kind, has dominated. The current fashion for bigger and bigger mergers is just the latest manifestation of this obsession. We may accept that quantity is not quality in virtually every other area of life, but in business organizations the two remain hopelessly intertwined and confused.

Now, those that are large are no longer in charge. In the mid-1970s, *Fortune 500* companies employed 20 percent of the US workforce. Today, that figure is less than 10 percent.[76] Similarly, companies with fewer than 19 employees account for 50 percent of US exports – the *Fortune 500* generates a mere 7 percent.[77]

Funky Inc. is small because, as pointed out by American commentator George Gilder, "The smaller the space; the larger the room."[78] We are creative in small teams. Maybe, the inhabitants of the Stone Age can teach us something. Back then, the average number of people in a tribe was some 40 individuals. On the African Savannah Plain 200,000 years ago, clans appeared to have had a maximum of around 150 members.[79] Nigel Nicholson of the London Business School points to "the persistent strength of small to mid-size family businesses throughout history. These companies, typically having no more than 150 members, remain the predominant model the world over, accounting for approximately 60 percent of all employment".

The optimum size of a company is a matter of perennial debate. Virgin chief Richard Branson argues that 50 to 60 people is enough. "If a company gets too large, break it into smaller parts. Once people start not knowing the people in the building and it starts to become impersonal, it's time to break up a company," he says. Bill Gates claims that around 200 is the maximum. Nathan Myhrvold, the R&D manager at Microsoft, says that eight people is about enough.[80] Although numbers vary, no one suggests that the 215,000 employees of a company like ABB is the optimum.

Of course, the mention of ABB is unfair. Together with GE, it has done more than virtually any other company to build small-ness into bigness. This is done through building the company around a number of levels. First, it has the dynamic working group consisting of some 2–5 individuals. Then it puts together 2–10 such groups into a dynamic business unit. How many such units can you have in a dynamic firm? Well, ABB claims to have approximately 5000 such profit centers – the average unit having some 45 employees. Still, even Jack Welch admits that while GE is the fastest elephant at the dance – it is still an elephant.[81]

> **"Once people start not knowing the people in the building and it starts to become impersonal, it's time to break up a company."**

Flatter

The funky firm is flatter. Flatter so that the time from problem detection to solution implementation is reduced. Chrysler, for instance, increased its span of control from 20 people per boss in the late 1980s to some 50. In the future, the organization hopes to reach 100.[82] The need to flatten the firm is hardly big news to any of you, but this might be. There are two very different ways of making a company flatter. The first is to take a sledgehammer and hit the organization on the top while simultaneously raising the lower levels by means of training and education. The second way is to take your hand, reach into the center of the organization and tear out the middle.

In the West we have had a preference for this second type of solution – getting rid of the middle. We all know how "boring and conservative" middle managers are. Now, we believe there is an inherent danger to this. We may end up relying on "seniles" managing "juveniles". Our experience is that often the best and most critical people sit in the middle. We just have to use them in the right way – as a value-adding link between the top and the bottom; translating vision into action and action into vision. Many Japanese companies no longer talk about bottom-up or top-down processes.[83] Instead, they realize that real organizational action is dependent on processes better characterized as middle-up-down.

⚎ Temporary

Funky Inc. is temporary. By this we mean working in projects and groups. Most of us know that teams are what Ed Lawler at the University of Southern California calls the Ferraris of organizational design. They are high performance, but also high maintenance and incredibly expensive.[84] Still, the changing circumstances of today's business world do not allow us to use one stable, unisex, one-size-fits-all structure. We have to be able to recombine our key assets and turn the firm into a team-park. To succeed, we need to institute a culture which mixes aspects of daring and sharing.

One of the principal problems relates to the fact that people will have to become used to no longer having a job. At funky firms people have many jobs. Today, the woman in the room next to you is your boss; tomorrow you are hers. Our careers are becoming more like those of actors. In the morning you are playing Macbeth, and later that day you are the Terminator. Naturally, this will cause serious problems for those who find security in having a piece of paper saying "job description" at the top. The new reality gives these people nightmares of Ingmar Bergman-esque proportions. One of the key tasks for leaders is to help people find themselves at ease with and enjoy this new situation.

➡ Horizontal

Funky firms work horizontally, in processes. The vertical hierarchical logic builds upon the simple assumption that the smart ones are located at the top and the stupid ones at the bottom. Hierarchy divides people into those who think and those who merely do. In reality, however, we know that most opportunities and problems in a company occur horizontally – across functions, business areas, divisions, or countries. Moreover, there is little room for suppliers and customers in a vertical logic – they sit outside the firm.

As long as the preferred strategy was addition, through acquisitions, mergers, and diversification, the natural principle for structuring the firm was that of division. However, when the hallmark of a competitive strategy shifts to subtraction, through focusing and outsourcing, the preferred structural denominator should be multiplication – combining stuff from different parts of the network into new customer offerings. This is just simple management by metrics.[85] If the main aim is to build an organization where the whole is greater than the sum of the parts, division is a highly inefficient method.

◎ Circular

All really fast systems, such as our brain, use circular design. This principle is perhaps more difficult to grasp. It builds on the fact that we have a tremendous ability to self-organize once we get 360-degree feedback. Circularity is about organizational democracy. At your company who appoints the CEO? The board, of course. Well, in most organizations marked by knowledge intensity this is the task of the other members of the firm. The other professors mostly elect the dean at a university. The other partners appoint the head at McKinsey and at most other consulting companies. This is also reflected in the shared ownership of the firm. The cardinals decide who becomes the Pope in the Catholic Church. (Letting the board decide could be somewhat problematic in the latter case.)

To check for circular qualities, we sometimes run a little experiment. We tell an audience that we want them to clap their hands in rhythm.[86] It only takes three or four claps before they are all in rhythm. Still, people did not have a boss. In fact, if they had had one, they would probably never ever get in rhythm. In that situation people would soon have lost track of who is the boss. And just what is he or she doing? Just as in real life. However, as long as we get feedback from all around, we are amazingly good at spontaneous coordination – provided that we have a shared understanding of the words "clap", "hands", and "in rhythm".

The experiment may sound ludicrous, but exchange those words for "global", "product", and "strategy". A shared language is critical for being able to manage without hierarchies. Otherwise we can have our meetings, make important decisions, and then realize that the other guys have abandoned the agreement claiming that it was a tactical rather than a strategic point, pertaining to the product concept, not the product itself.

◀ Open

Unfortunately, simply changing internal structures won't suffice. Given that the firm is narrower and hollower, we also need to develop abilities to become increasingly networked. For Focused Inc. the future will mean more joint ventures, strategic alliances and partnerships. Not all assets can be kept internally. The network, rather than the single firm, is becoming the relevant unit of analysis and action. Cooperate with customers, suppliers, *and* competitors. Corporate adultery becomes OK, when you really need the skills and resources of a competitor. Business is not a zero-sum game. This calls for a new type of logic. As noted by Professor Robert Axelrod, "In zero-sum games you always try to hide your strategy but in non-zero-sum games you might want to announce your strategy in public so the other players need to adapt to it."[87]

> **Corporate adultery becomes OK, when you really need the skills and resources of a competitor.**

It's our network/supply chain against the others. The Seven-Up/RC bottling company brews arch competitors Lipton and Arizona ice-tea in the same tanks.[88] The Volvo S40 and Mitsubishi Carisma are both built in the same factory in Ghent, Holland. Two rivals under the same roof. But keep in mind the quality of your partners and the relationships is heavily contingent on your own attractiveness and willingness to give as well as take.

▤ MEASURED

Control freaks of the world do not despair. Control will not disappear. It will only become more indirect. We do not foresee that the main use of IT for a lot of organizations will lie in increasing communication, coordination, customization, and external contacts. Instead, information systems will be used to increase control by measuring more things, new things, at multiple levels, and at a greater frequency than before. To a certain extent, this is a substitute for the loss of hierarchical control resulting from the introduction of new structures.

How many firms really measure not only their own but also their customers' market and mindshare? Are these guys the fastest-growing in their industries? How many companies systematically organize knowledge about their competitors and suppliers? How many firms measure things such as innovation, employee stuff, attractiveness, human exports, company demographics, environmental impact, and so on? How many companies measure their return on knowledge (ROK), return on decency (ROD) or return on people (ROP)? And just who is responsible for measuring all these new things?

We need appropriate goals. The sophisticated companies of today use stretch goals, goals that challenge people to perform beyond what they thought was possible. At Toshiba the stretch goal for a VCR was to make it with half the number of parts, in half the time and at half the cost.[89] Stretch goals are general. You do not tell the experts how to do it – you provide a challenging benchmark. Now, this is easier said than done. Not only are these goals hard to attain, it is also difficult to set them. It is difficult because we all have psychological limitations. Most of us know that the present way of doings things is not perfect, but we do believe that we are fairly close to the optimal solution. It is tricky to pose goals that almost seem ridiculous and unattainable.

Management thinker Charles Handy tells the story of Ford Motors, which experienced exactly this problem when deciding to lay off 100 people at the accounts receivable department.[90] People screamed, "We just about managed to do this with 500 employees, how are we supposed to manage with only 400?" It took some time, but finally the company had done it. Champagne bottles were opened and everyone was happy. Some time later the company launched a major benchmarking project, in which the goal was to study the Japanese competitor Mazda. The Ford people were surprised to find that Mazda had only five employees in its equivalent department. Ford had to rethink its way of operating. Finally, it managed to come down from 400 employees to 100.

Why did Ford not set this goal from the beginning? The answer is psychological precincts. Such improvements seemed impossible within the existing paradigm. A lot of people would say that if you believe that you can do it with 100 people, then you must have been pretty stupid using 500. For protection, we lock on a certain logic. To make real changes we have got to rethink our basic assumptions and break free from the logic of the past. We need what Konusuke Matsushita used to call, "Torawarenai sunao-na kokoro" – a mind that does not stick.

A recipe for success?

So you have focused, leveraged your competences in all imaginable directions, created an innovative company that is anything but hierarchically organized. But are these changes adequate? Is this the recipe for future success? Short answer: NO! All the

Do not compete!

changes that we have proposed – all the traits of Funky Inc. – are merely necessary but not sufficient for securing future success.

But they are necessary. Very necessary. The problem is that all companies are doing it. All organizations are refocusing, realigning, renewing, reorganizing, re-engineering, etc.

The word competition comes from Latin and literally means "seeking together" or "choosing to run in the same race". But in an age of abundance the tracks are pretty crowded. The others are constantly stepping on your toes, pushing and elbowing you, trying to get to the customers first. So, and slightly paradoxically, the only (un)reasonable thing to do is *not* to compete. As soon as we start running alongside all the others, in our pursuit of marketshare, mindshare, or whatever-share, we risk ending up as one in the crowd – invisible to the customers. When we take part in the same race for top talent as all the others it is hard for people to tell the difference.

The dirty little secret of market capitalism in all its many forms is that successful companies have become so by killing the spirit of free enterprise. They have all succeeded in creating monopolies, at least for a short moment in time. Competitiveness comes about by not competing. Success arises from being different. And then being prepared to change again.

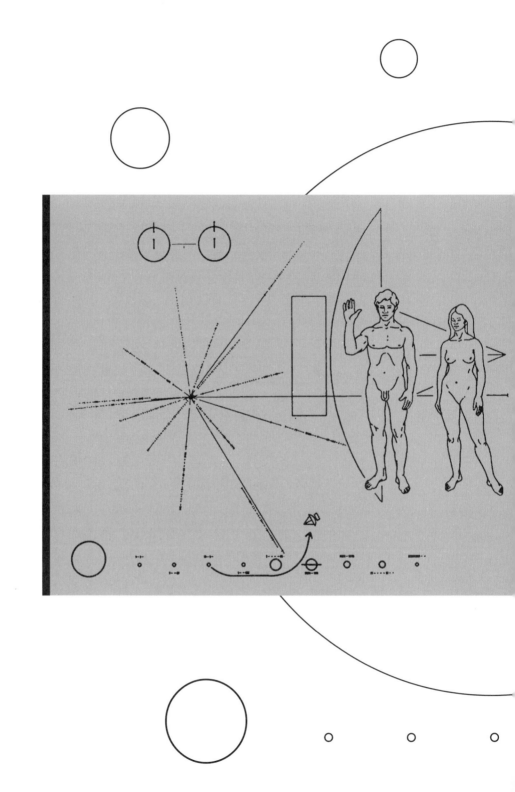

Funky U

5

"We must be the change we
wish to see in the world"

MAHATMA GANDHI

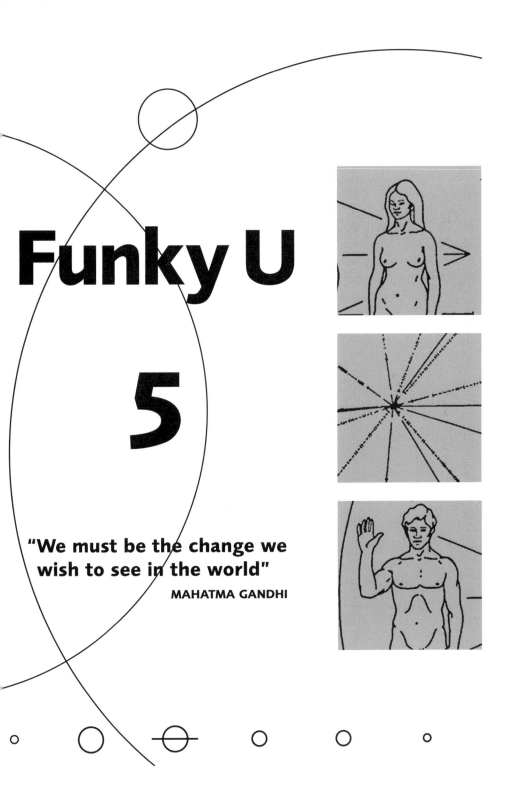

Shopping and fucking.

Shopping and fucking are the only things left.

Shopping and fucking shape the dreams of our times.

Shopping and fucking, says controversial British playwright Mark Ravenhill, are the only things that really motivate the younger generation. Shopping and fucking are what really get their juices flowing.

So, you might then ask, who are the leaders of these champions of retailing and copulation? In many cases, they are middle-aged men who probably haven't had steaming sex since the late 1970s and who leave the shopping to the rest of the family.

Over the top? Excessive? Perhaps. But, even if Mark Ravenhill is only 25 percent right – indeed even if he is only 10 percent right – we had better come up with new ways to organize our companies, new ways to capture the attention of demanding customers, *and* new ways to treat our colleagues – peers, bosses and subordinates. We have to motivate them in new ways, find new ways to evaluate and reward them, train them, inspire them, and lead them. In the funky village, people do not get their kicks from celibacy and savings.

In the funky village, people do not get their kicks from celibacy and savings.

Never forget or underestimate how strongly celibacy and saving were enshrined in previous eras. In the old world, peopled saved, as they still do in Japan – the only country where people have to be given money and told to go shopping – because it was the route to betterment. Similarly, celibacy was the route to spiritual improvement. These two pillars of the old world are crumbling. Leisure and pleasure are the new reality. Instant gratification is expected. Fucking and shopping. Freud and Jung (in that order) set loose.

The legacy of self-motivation left by Martin Luther is now being cast off. The self-motivated employee used to wake up every morning eager to go to work – praying by working. Then, one day, he or she just decided to stay in bed. Today, people work to get rich, to have fun, to meet new people, see new places and

Martin Luther is dead x Karl Marx was right = mega-challenges for the modern manager

be seen, to develop themselves, or whatever. But, they no longer work out of moral obligation. Work is no longer automatically accepted as a good thing. Motivation is no longer taken for granted. We've moved from *have to* to *want to*.

If you combine the fact that Martin Luther's tenets and assumptions are dead with the fact that Karl Marx was right, things take on a radically different appearance. Martin Luther is dead x Karl Marx was right = mega-challenges for the modern manager (as well as society in general). Suddenly the organization is – from the individual's perspective – disposable rather than permanent. Today, people hire organizations, rather than vice versa. Says former presidential advisor Robert Reich, "It is a seller's market for talent. People can afford to shop around for the right boss ... the right environment. In the old economy it was a buyer's market ... It was why hire? Now why join up?"[1]

In the long run, Charles Handy claims that this also means that the main task of the company will no longer be to employ people, as it once was. The key task will be to organize.[2] Clearly, there is a huge difference between being a great employer and a great organizer.

The organizer offers opportunities rather than jobs – a creative space. An organizer has to take an idea, identify the resources required to make it happen, then attract those resources. An inspired organizer can mobilize armies of intellectual mercenaries overnight to solve a specific problem.

In the organizing paradigm, nothing is given. Tasks may change. It is temporary, a potent and unstable fusion of ideas and people. Risk, dynamism and constant value creation are the driving forces of organizing. Leaders must create forcefields – magnets that suck in talent, rather than having permanent employees sucking up to them.

Stars attract stars; losers pull in losers. We are all players in the great global attraction game.

The organizing paradigm means that the legal boundaries of the firm are of less and less importance. It is the operational boundary that counts. The leader handles an array of partners and collaborators, network upon network. It's The United Firms of Unilever rather than Unilever. Inspiration must be provided to the extended family/the network and only the best will do. There is more: these individuals/firms have alternatives each and every minute of each and every day. People have to be treated like celebrities. They are Hollywood stars or sports stars, demanding prima donnas. Upset them at your peril. Lose one and they will all go. Stars attract stars; losers pull in losers. We are all players in the great global attraction game. Individuals are players. Companies are players and regions are players. At the end of the day – Silicon Valley is nothing more and nothing less than a pretty attractive place inhabited by some pretty attractive organizations and individuals.

In such a world, fundamentally different demands are imposed on leaders – and this applies to political and religious leaders as well as those in business. In fact, it applies to all leaders – boy scout leaders, sports coaches, directors, union representatives, and so on.

Meaningful leadership

Mobilizing forces is no longer straightforward. People don't snap to attention. They don't passively fall into line. When power is in the hands of the people, intimidation and threats do not work. And, if they do work, you are dead because this means you hired the wrong people.

People are everything. Remember that even someone like Neutron Jack Welch of GE personally interviews all candidates for the top 500 jobs at the company and admits that his whole job is "picking the right people".[3] Bill Gates also dedicates a lot of time to attracting the most talented people to his company. There is nothing new in this – the best leaders have been spending time on recruitment for decades, if not centuries. King Arthur did it. Cosimo di Medici did it. Duke Ellington did it. Ronald Reagan did it.

The word management comes from Italian "maneggio/maneggiare" and the French word "manège", the training ring in which horses run around encouraged by a long whip held by the horse trainer. But what if the horses learned to run around by themselves? What if the horses actually do a better job at running around without the trainer, age 46.5, holding a whip and standing in the middle? Or, what if the horses have even figured out that in a surplus society with complete global competition there are probably more sensible things to do than to keep on running around in circles. If you try to break-in smart people, they will break-out.

People may no longer be so obedient, but that does not mean that leadership is redundant. On the contrary, the funky world requires limitless leadership. This will not involve our traditional notion of a leader. Not that traditional leaders ever really existed – real leaders exist only in the heads and hearts of those who believe in them.

The trouble is that modern management is often built on the assumption that the absence of leadership results in chaos. The nightmare is pyromaniac leadership in a firm inhabited by corporate arsonists constantly threatening the well-being of the company. In this nightmare, the task of the leader is simply to put out the fires. Top management team = fire department.

We do not believe that putting out fires is the job of the leader. Nor is it the task of the leader to bring order to chaos. Take leadership away and you do not automatically get corporate chaos desperately in need of firm leadership. Take leadership away and you usually get repetition and reproduction. The organization becomes constipated, incapable of self-renewal.

Instead, a major role of leaders, anywhere and everywhere, is to infuse chaos into order. Rather than hunting down pyromaniacs, we are talking about prophylactic leadership. The main aim is to make yourself abundant. Leaders = midwives. Leaders must **Funky leaders are creators** challenge people to depart from **of chaos as much** the patterns of the past and to **as originators of order.** destroy the present profit-makers by creating new ones. *Meaningful* leadership is about stirring the pot rather than putting on the lid. Funky leaders are creators of chaos as much as originators of order. It is the job of great leaders – not only *the* leader – to support the organization in combining order and chaos.

From the point of view of those being led, a group to which we all belong at certain times, four critical requirements of funky leaders will arise: increased calls for direction and tolerance, attraction and attention.

Direction – spin me

Direction is not a matter of command and control, but of focusing, allowing and encouraging people to focus on what really matters. It is spiritual management rather than micro-management. In a chaotic world, people cry out for individuals who can provide meaning for their private and professional lives. There remains a perpetual need for guidance. Guidance is manifested through formulating and clarifying underlying assumptions about the world, our capabilities and what we want to happen. These assumptions are the existential foundation of any business. All organizations need a shared idea of why they exist, who they are, and where to go. In modern businesses this is usually expressed through a vision. The problem is that most companies do not have an operationally potent vision. Instead, most are generic wish lists, the length of which is only matched by their emptiness – *wish ons*. Visions should be unique. They should differentiate.

In practice, visions often tend to be vacuums. People frequently tell us that the vision of their firm is to make money. But is this really unique? Do all their competitors focus on losing money?

At Disney the vision is to "make people happy" and at Motorola it is "wireless". 3M focuses on "solving unsolved problems". AT&T talks about IM&M –"information movement and management".

All visions should be able to survive a triviality test. If it sounds stupid when you negate it – our vision is not to make money – go back to square one and try again.

To provide direction, a vision should be clear, continuous, and consistent.[4] It should inspire commitment and be continually communicated. Funky leaders communicate, then communicate the same thing again, and again, and again. They never grow tired or, at least, never appear to grow tired.

Scott McNealy of Sun Microsystems has a favorite formula: 0.6L. Every time information passes a layer in the organization only 60 percent gets through. This quickly adds up – especially in hierarchical firms with an excessive number of layers. Once you have tried informing people the first time, maybe one percent have got it. When you believe you have 90 percent on board, perhaps 10 percent are beginning to understand. As Percy Barnevik puts it, "You don't inform, you over-inform."

We need to over-inform not because people are stupid, but because people have other, more important things on their mind, such as their kids, vacation and the up-coming visit from their mother-in-law. Work matters but it is never the only thing. And if it is, once again, you should question if these rather one-dimensional obsessives are the right people for your business.

Truth be told, many managers need to over-inform because they have made such a bad job of communicating in the past that there is a huge reservoir of skepticism and cynicism directed at any talk of visions and missions. People know from experience that visions do not matter and that another will be along in a year or two.

With the onus on communication, leaders are spin-doctors. Their job is to be general *and* overly precise. It is an impossible paradox but one which they have to make possible. Essentially, they distill the company direction into the most potent capsule. At Disney the vision is to "make people happy" and at Motorola it is "wireless". 3M focuses on "solving unsolved problems". AT&T talks about IM&M – "information movement and management". These statements are simple enough to be shared by all employees, and they are clear in saying what the companies should *not* be doing. Try showing up at Motorola with a wire and see what happens. Can you say this about your organization's vision?

As well as visionary bullets, we also need more short-term oriented goals that inspire change and that themselves change over time. Jim Collins and Jerry Porras in their book *Built to Last*, call such things big hairy audacious goals (BHAGs).[5] These come in many shapes and forms. They can be quantitative or qualitative. In the early 1990s, US retailer Wal-Mart set its aim on "becoming a $125 billion company by the year 2000". In contrast, almost 100 years ago Ford decided to "democratize the automobile". BHAGs can be geared toward a common enemy, such as Nike's "Crush Adidas" from the 1960s, or they can use role models as a benchmark. In the 1940s Stanford University decided to try to "become the Harvard of the West". A more inwardly oriented focus was used by General Electric in its 1980s goal: "Become number one or two in every market we serve and revolutionize this company to have the strengths of a big company combined with the agility of a small company."

As well as being the distilled essence of what a company is and what a company stands for, visions and goals should also ignite and inspire commitment. People must want to belong. They must be banging on your door to sign up. Simply and powerfully, the International Red Cross is there "to serve the most vulnerable". Do you really feel a tingle or see tears in the eyes of your colleagues when you discuss your company's vision?

Communicating a vision not only involves repetition and a carefully distilled message; it demands the ability to tell a story. True leaders are CSOs – Chief Storytelling Officers. They provide the focus, inspiration and meaning that the organization has been crying out for. The Danish children's book author Hans Christian Andersen is probably, at times, more useful in the corporate trenches than management prophet Peter Drucker.

True leaders are CSOs – Chief Storytelling Officers.

Metaphors and language are incredibly powerful. Indeed, language shapes and reshapes the world around us. It can reassure – words such as "airport" and "Internet", for example, are combinations of old words used to describe new phenomena – and it can help create a new world. Stories and myths contain a built-in tension that draws people in and ensures that the message sticks. They are adaptable, open to an array of interpretations, and are universal and eternal. They communicate more than mere facts.

Look at the major religious texts – the Bible, the Koran, Bhagavad-Gita, etc. They communicate wisdom through metaphors, stories and analogies. And when rules are used, they tend to be short and snappy. In the Old Testament, God tells Moses to apply a mere 10 commandments rather than a complex plethora of rules and regulations. The advice for the modern-day manager is to go for the generic – do not try to nail down all the specifics. Put your trust in the good judgment of people.

Funky leaders give rise to and spread stories. They communicate messages through the stories that they tell and which emerge around them. At ABB, there is the famous story of two people from the opposite sides of the matrix asking Percy Barnevik if he could resolve a problem for them. Barnevik said he would be pleased to do so, but only once. If they came back with another problem, they would both be fired. The message was unequivocal – take responsibility and sort out your problems – and the story quickly became part of ABB folklore.

At IKEA, the company founder, Ingvar Kamprad uses storytelling. For example, many know the story of Kamprad travelling by bus to and from airports to save money. It is a simple story, easily told in a single sentence, but its ramifications and its message are very powerful. Here is a rich man who is still in touch with reality, who is concerned with value, who is the same as us. Kamprad's bus journeys are a metaphor of the values embodied by IKEA. The other thing about stories is that few care if they are true or not. Myths outweigh facts.

Applying management by stories also means that the leader is held to ransom by the organization. Management by rules allows managers to use a set of differentiated and people-specific standards. It is OK for executives to travel business class, but those not part of the top management team still need to save money on paper-clips. But when we communicate generic insights through stories the ramifications of divergent behavior are great. Kamprad in a cab? No way. Nor can he order champagne and caviar; or stay at the Peninsula in Hong Kong or the George V in Paris. He is condemned to stay at middle-ranking hotels and to ride on buses. Any champagne must be consumed behind closed curtains – and in a transparent society all curtains are made of clear plastic.

The message is simple: light the camp fire, gather the tribe, and start preaching and practicing. Lift us up where we belong.

Experimentation – forgive me

Business life has, until now, been built around spurts of creation and extended periods of exploitation. Companies exploited natural resources, exploited technologies and exploited people. We are good at exploitation because we have hundreds, not to say thousands, of years of experience. We know exactly what to do when we find a gold mine. We put structures and systems in place and get to work. When it is exhausted we look for the next gold mine.

In contrast, we are not very good at creation. Our societies are not built for it. Our organizations are not designed for it. And most people are not trained for it.

By its very nature, creation involves a departure from traditional structures and frames. In a world of creativity-sucking board meetings, past structures have ruled the roost. Now, we have to be prepared to depart from the agenda. Creativity also demands the introduction of some new structures. Creation is not, repeat not, anarchical.

Pursuing other routes than the one most traveled can prove worth while. Get off the beaten track. After all, Viagra was discovered when the scientists were looking to develop a drug to relieve high blood pressure; Columbus was actually trying to reach India rather than America; and Fleming's penicillin was the result of a "failed" experiment, as was galvanized rubber.

An innovative environment must have an exceptionally high tolerance for mistakes.

To survive in the surplus society we need more innovation. Innovation means creating what is not. Innovation is about creating things the world hasn't seen before. Innovation is about asking "What if ... ?" then asking it again, and again, and again. This partly explains why entrepreneurs are sometimes difficult to deal with. While most journalists, academics, managers and civil servants deal with what is, these people do exactly the opposite.

Innovation requires experimentation. Experiments are risky. We can succeed or fail. So, an innovative environment must have an exceptionally high tolerance for mistakes. And so must leaders of innovative organizations. In a sense, failure lies at the very heart of a market economy. In experimentation, we should forgive while never forgetting what we have learned. According to

Deepak Sethi of AT&T, the organization of tomorrow will actually *demand* mistakes and failures.[6] We have got to fail faster to learn quicker and succeed sooner. "Failure is just part of the culture of innovation. Accept it and become stronger," advises Albert Yu, Senior Vice-President at Intel.[7] In Silicon Valley, failure is not a black dot – it is a badge of achievement.[8]

The trouble is that traditional organizations are not the most forgiving of environments. In many firms, failure carries the corporate equivalent of the death penalty. If you make a mistake, corporate Siberia beckons. This sends a signal to the corporate system that failure is punished. This not only stops people from failing – it stops them from trying. It leads to the building of systems that act against innovation rather than ones that nurture innovation.

True innovators are prepared to fail in pursuit of unknown territories – *terra incognita* instead of *terra firma.* The pursuit of difference and creativity involves astonishing twists and turns. During the last century, the success of Mahatma Gandhi's India, Henry Ford's Model T, Man Ray's photographs, Ruben Rausing's TetraPak, the Beatles' Sgt Pepper's album, the Fosbery flop in athletics and Akito Morita's Sony Walkman can all be attributed to their unusual ability to combine new technology, institutions and values in unexpected ways. They took risks. They surprised people and, probably, themselves.

Jesus took risks and was crucified

Some risk their lives in pursuit of creating something new and different. The great value innovator Jesus took risks and was crucified. In our times, Nelson Mandela took risks and almost died for it. Alfred Nobel took risks and passed away in solitude. Van Gogh took risks, was ridiculed and committed suicide. For every Bill Gates and Michael Dell, or any other well-known, risk-prone explorer, there are thousands and thousands of others who tried

Alfred Nobel took risks and passed away in solitude

and failed. They lost their families, friends, fortunes, dignity and sometimes, ultimately, their lives. Our thoughts should go out to all those forgotten heroes who tried and failed. We should hail them, because the innermost mechanism of human progress is called failure. If it were not for all the fools trying to do the impossible – over and over again – we would still be living in caves.

Traditionalists should remember that the only way not to fail is not to try. And try we must. No failures; no development. Philosopher Ludwig Wittgenstein even argued that, "If people never did silly things, nothing intelligent would ever happen."

Respect is therefore due to all who take risks. Companies must become breeding grounds of risk takers. To do so requires a huge shift. In military action, great importance is attached to taking care of the wounded and seeking out those missing in action. How else could you keep morale up? In the French Foreign Legion you receive a medal if you are wounded. Taking reasonable, calculated risks (a classical contradiction in terms) is what you are there for. If the wounded were quickly shunted away and ignored as failures, morale would plummet. Yet, that is what happens in many organizations.

But not in all. Think, for example, of two corporate disasters. First, one of the most talked about corporate mishaps of the modern era: the 1985 decision by Coca-Cola to replace its traditional recipe cola with New Coke. In detailed research it had discovered that most consumers preferred the new recipe. It was, they said, smoother, sweeter and preferable to the old version. This conveniently overlooked the fact that the old version was selling in many millions every day of the week. It also overlooked the fact that people who buy a Coke buy something more and something else than the mere atoms. To call this the marketing own goal of the century would be to understate the effect only slightly. Coke was faced with a barrage of criticism. On the other hand, its arch rival Pepsi could barely contain its glee – indeed, it quickly produced advertising which was extremely gleeful, rubbing in the fact that "the real thing" remained unchanged.

Realizing that its move had been disastrous, Coke backtracked and, after 90 days, re-introduced the original coke. It has not been tinkered with since. So, did heads roll? Did the Coca-Cola chief, Roberto Goizueta, immediately head to the door marked exit? No. In fact, not a single person from the management team left because of the New Coke disaster.[9]

Second, there was GE's experience with Kidder Peabody. Big bucks were lost and the deal remains one of the few blemishes on GE chief Jack Welch's record. In 1986 GE bought 80 percent of Kidder Peabody for $600 million. The Kidder debacle cost GE $1.2 billion. "I've rewarded failures by giving out awards to people when they've failed, because they took a swing," says Welch. "Keep taking swings. I teach a course at Crotonville (the GE training center) for six hours – four to six hours – on leadership. I always say, if the chairman can buy Kidder Peabody and mess it up, you can do about anything. It was on the front page of *The Wall Street Journal* 19 times. Now, if the chairman can do that and still survive, you ought to be able to take swings everywhere. You can hardly do worse."[10]

Welch claims to have built a culture in which failure is accepted as a positive thing. "Punishing failure assures that no one dares," he contends.[11] His emphasis is on taking risks and learning from them if things go wrong.

Similarly, the CEO of one major US corporation handed out

awards for Best Failures during his senior executive forum. Jaws dropped at the very thought. This represented a major cultural shift in that, only a year before, failures – especially big or public ones – were to be hidden not celebrated.

It is a fact that the most intensive learning experiences tend to occur when we fail rather than when we succeed. "Most of the things I have learnt were not learned formally but through accidents and failure. I learned from small catastrophes," admits Charles Handy.[12] He is not alone. Most of us learn in such a haphazard and occasionally unhappy way. If there were awards for Best Failures we would have a large number to choose from.

Failure happens. Give people trust and it will happen more productively. We are not saying that leaders should promote risk-taking *per se*. Rather, it is a question of making it less risky to take risks. Work at Decision Research, a company based in Eugene, Oregon studying risk management strategies, suggests that people are more likely to accept risks if they perceive them to be voluntarily undertaken, controllable, understandable and equally distributed. And, conversely, people are less willing to take risks that they don't understand and which are unfairly distributed.[13]

Failure happens. Give people trust and it will happen more productively.

Give people freedom and they will pursue their own creative byways. Give people time and you don't know what creative results will emerge – slack is a prerequisite for innovation. 3M does just that with its 15 percent policy – researchers can spend up to 15 percent of their time on their own projects. The 15 percent policy is called, among other things, "the bootleg policy". It may also be called a competitive advantage because it has helped foster and nurture so many good ideas – most notably the Post-it.

The 15 percent policy encourages researchers to roam further afield. Hajime Mitari, the President of Canon, has said, "We should do something when people say it is crazy. If people say something is good, it means that someone else is already doing it."[14] Along similar lines, Nobel Laureate Arno Penzias of Bell

Labs says, "The definition of a lousy product is one that has no enemies within the company."[15]

The aim should be the creation of a bubbling ferment of ideas. "The object is to spur as many ideas as possible because perhaps 1 in 1000 will turn out to fit," explains Post-it Note developer, Art Fry.[16] "An idea might be a perfectly good idea for another company, but not for yours. Putting together a new product is like putting together a jigsaw puzzle such as raw material suppliers, distributors, government regulations and the amount of capital you have to spend. If one part doesn't fit, the whole project can fail. Your work might have been brilliant but somebody else dropping the ball can lead to failure."

And, in an age of abundance, no organization or leader can rest on their laurels. Innovation means competing with yourself. The key message sent to product development teams in Silicon Valley is "Obsolete your own products". Most companies do not need more CEOs – they need a couple of CDOs, chief destruction officers, people who destroy the old cash cows by creating new ones.[17] If you are not willing to commit to this act of creative destruction, rest assured that your competitors are. We better start eating our lunches before someone else does. Or, as Adam Smith put it more than 200 years ago, "It takes a lot of ruin to make the wealth of a great nation."[18] The same reasoning applies to all companies, regardless of age, size, industry, and geographical origin.

Education – develop me

In a brain-based world, we have to change our definition of education and training. We used to believe in taking a huge overdose of education until the age of 25. The theory was that this massive infusion of education would keep us high and flying for the next 40 years or so, and after that no one would need us any more.

This approach to learning means that for the majority of people's lives learning wasn't even on their agenda. It was generic and wide-ranging rather than personalized and targeted. It overlooked the fact that education is not about filling people's heads with facts. It is emotion and soul. It is personal.

In a world where competitive advantages can be found in softwhere, education needs to be continuous and lifelong. Education is a competitive weapon – for individuals as well as firms. The workplace has to become a campus. If you want to attract and retain the best people, you will have to train them. Or, as James Sims, CEO at Cambridge Technology Partners, puts it, "Most people will have seven jobs before their career is over. What they look for in an employer is a continuous investment in their career."[19] Sims' company spends 7 percent of sales on training – 18 times more than the average US firm.

The reality is that employee education isn't growing 100 percent faster than academia, but 100 times or 10,000 percent faster.[20] Companies such as Apple, SiliconGraphics, and Intel have already institutionalized sabbaticals for their top employees. You are allowed to retreat for as long as one year to further your skills.

Already companies are setting up their own "universities" to train tomorrow's executives. There are now 1200 corporate universities worldwide covering virtually every industry.[21] On the surface these are not institutions which the denizens of Harvard are likely to lose sleep over. McDonalds' Hamburger University in Oak Brook, Illinois lacks academic *gravitas.* But, over 35 years it has produced more than 50,000 graduates and has 30 resident professors delivering programs in 22 languages.[22]

Skeptics may shake their heads at the very idea of Hamburger University or Disney University, but the rate at which corporate universities are opening suggests that major corporations take them very seriously. Perhaps the best-known corporate university is that run by Motorola. The Motorola University, "an instrument of renewal" according to the company, supplies 550,000 student days a year and costs $170 million.[23] Every single Motorola employee – and there are 139,000 – is expected to receive at least 40 hours of training per year. The company has also developed its own international MBA program. Motorola calculates that every dollar invested in training reaps $33.[24]

Corporate universities are not solely an US phenomenon. In April 1998, British Aerospace unveiled plans to create its own virtual university, called the British Aerospace Virtual University, in partnership with outside academic institutions. In the next decade, it pledged to invest more than £1.5 billion in building the company's "knowledge base".

Changing educational needs will produce changing educational institutions. "Universities won't survive. The future is outside the traditional campus, outside the traditional classroom. Distance learning is coming on fast," says no less a sage than Peter Drucker. While futurists Stan Davis and Jim Botkin predict "the school house of the future may be neither school nor house".[25]

Technology is revolutionizing education. Traditional institutions, such as universities and business schools, have done nothing while upstarts have stolen a march. Soon even bigger corporations will become involved in education. When media group, Pearson bought Simon & Schuster's education, reference and business and professional publishing activities for $3.6 billion in 1998, education was the top of its agenda. "Education is one of the great growth industries of our time," pronounced Pearson's Chief Executive, Marjorie Scardino. Companies such as Microsoft, Disney, and News Corporation are also eyeing the opportunities. Michael Milken, the junk bond king who was eventually imprisoned, is now out and investing heavily in any business which combines education and technology. He has seen the future.

We have to turn the workplace into a gas station for our brains, not only a racetrack.

Amid this welcome and overdue maelstrom of activity, the nature of education has fundamentally changed and will continue to do so. Learning is now increasingly regarded as lifelong – though exactly what this means or entails is often a little vague – and it is also regarded as personal.

As a lot of knowledge is tacit and difficult to communicate, learning can by no means be restricted to the "classroom". We must also learn on the job. We have to turn the workplace into a gas station for our brains, not only a racetrack. Development and education is as much about improving the processes in which we work and getting to know the people around us as it is about reading yet another book or listening to another lecture. Development is about mentoring, training disciples and coaching. It is the job of leaders to create new leaders. Leadership is about contaminating and being contaminated with knowledge. The distinction between learning, working and living is gone – it is one and the same thing.

Personalization – see me

Today, most companies excel in responding to complaints, requests and all other whimsies from core customers. They do so in a few hours or sometimes even a few minutes. Yet, suggestions and questions from core competents – the stars, who don't happen to be top managers – are often not even taken seriously. And, as once noted by the founder of Wal-Mart, Sam Walton, it does not take more than a week or two before employees start treating the customers the same way the employer is treating them.[26] Then, remember what Larry Bossidy at Allied Signal, says, "At the end of the day we bet on people, not strategies."[27]

At your firm, are the employees treated as investors? Because this is what they are – intellectual investors. Every day they bring their heads and hearts to work. And if they don't, you will soon be extinct. We must treat our people like volunteers. Maybe we should ask the Red Cross or the Salvation Army to share their secrets with us?

The only thing that now makes capital dance is talent.

And any lack of attention is more problematic for the firm than for the individual members. The organization is disposable – the stars will keep on shining. If, for one reason or another, CNN goes down the drain, it's not detrimental to Larry King. If Alessi goes bankrupt – designer Philippe Starck may shed a tear, but soon he's back on track. If Harvard Business School has to close down the store, Professor Rosabeth Moss Kanter just moves on. If Warner is teetering on the abyss, the artist formerly known as Prince is unlikely to have sleepless nights. In an age where capital is abundant, the bargaining power of Larry, Philippe, Rosabeth and the Symbol is increasing by the hour, by the minute, by the second. The only thing that now makes capital dance is talent. And it's not every second dance – capital is engaged in a non-stop St Vitus dance.

People differ

Human beings are not bulk goods. They come in different shapes and forms. Each and every individual is different. Every now and then this is brought to our attention. But change takes time. It took the car industry close to 100 years to realize that women are not small men. In the funky fragmented village, we can look forward to further differentiation of individuals and their needs. One-to-one everything.

You either manage this differentiation or you watch as your most precious assets walk out of the door. If you educate people and then treat them as morons or just a human resource, the best ones will leave. Education without personalization treats training as a cost rather than an investment.

To attract and retain good men and women we have to treat them as individuals. The word *individual* originates from Latin and literally means indivisible. We are moving toward one-to-one leadership. The consequence is that each and every little system needs to be personalized. People can be treated and approached, evaluated and rewarded, motivated and inspired in a number of different ways. At the companies voted most popular to work for in the US, the employees are offered things such as on-the-job massages, dry cleaning or a personal concierge. We are all unique individuals. Dress code at Sun Microsystems = you must.

The highly successful software company SAS Institute in North Carolina has no limits on sick days. You can even stay home to take care of sick family members. The firm is responsible for the largest daycare operations in the state. People work a 35-hour week and there are baby seats in the lunchroom.[28] Pampering? Sure, but if you can't pamper your own people, you are hardly likely to pamper your customers and go that extra mile to enhance their experience.

People differ and what motivates them differs

People are motivated by different things, in different ways, and at different times. What motivates you does not motivate us, and what motivates your colleagues does not necessarily motivate you. To prevent total chaos, funky organizations must appeal to a tribe of people with some commonality in attitude. Think about the cases of SouthWest Airlines and McKinsey. The lowest common denominator allows us to differ in another dimension. So, some people may say, "But I don't work with my friends – those who share my vibes." Well, do you want to change employer or friends?

Increasingly motivation is based on values rather than cash.

And these values are not inevitably concerned with money. Not for all people. "Too many organizations seem to believe that the only motivation to work is an economic one. Treating knowledge assets like Skinnerian rats is hardly the way to get the best out of people," says strategy guru Gary Hamel.[29] Instead of being provided with detailed job descriptions, employees should provide managers with motivation descriptions.

In the well-known Maslowian hierarchy of needs, we all start at the bottom with satisfying our hunger and then slowly move toward self-realization. Today, things are turned upside down. Many people go for self-realization first – then the rest. They are prepared to starve for a few weeks to be able to buy a piece of art, a BMW mountain bike (they do exist and are predictably expensive), a new pair of Air-Jordans from Nike, or to travel to the Himalayas.

Increasingly motivation is based on values rather than cash. Historically, loyalty was basically bought. The employer offered gradual progression up the hierarchy, a decent salary and job security. In return, the employee offered unwavering loyalty and a hard day's work. Now, values determine loyalty. "Every organization needs values, but a lean organization needs them even more," GE's Jack Welch says. "When you strip away the support systems of staffs and layers, people have to change their habits and expectations, or else the stress will just overwhelm them."[30] The challenge for organizations is that values are more complex than mere money. Values cannot be simplistically condensed into a mission statement or neatly printed on an embossed card. And values cannot be invented. Either we have them or we don't.

By having and communicating a clear set of values, the organization becomes self-selecting – it primarily attracts people who share that attitude. Being fuzzy means that anyone or no one will knock on the door. Remember that it is a buyer's market. The competents are in charge. For stars there is a choice. They work for companies that are in accord with their own value systems. If they don't want to work for a polluter, they will not. After all, people want to hold their heads up when they are with their peers. They don't want an embarrassed silence when they announce whom they work for. "These days we value a great mission and a great working lifestyle as much as a bigger desk and the prospect of promotion," says Publisher, Richard Stagg. "Who gets out of bed in the morning for a distant corporate objective? If a company gives real meaning to people's work and the freedom and resources to pursue their ideas then it's a good place to be."[31]

If people differ and their motivations differ, rewards must differ

We are used to differentiated contracts in every other market but not in the labor market. While standard contracts are acceptable in a mass production context they are hardly applicable to a building full of highly charged brains with widely different reasons for being there. Celebrities want customized working hours, rewards, perks, office furniture and so on. And not only global executives qualify as celebrities. We are talking about janitors, programmers, teachers and sales reps – anyone who is really good at what he or she is doing.

We live in a world in which working contracts are increasingly individual and individualistic. People will express themselves through their contracts. You are your contract, and your contract is you. The Brazilian soccer player, Edmundo, has written into his contract with Italian team Fiorentina that he has a two-week vacation during the Rio Carnival. Excessive? Perhaps it is, but what if it maximizes his performance during the rest of the football season?

The emerging system will have to share the profits with its talents. We are moving toward an outright star system. We trade in talents and, as a result, can expect **You are your contract,** much more sophisticated and diverse **and your contract is you.** contracts between single individuals and business firms. Business-to-business contracts are in most cases tailor made. Transaction-specific. Brains and their owners are not homogeneous. They are unique, so the transaction-specificity increases. This must be reflected in employment contracts.

People differ and the only way you will find out how much they differ is by listening to them

Blind loyalty is undoubtedly dead. Corporate man is now as likely to be corporate woman. "Passive obedience was once mistaken for loyalty. The entire notion of loyalty was wrapped up with control. Now, people are not loyal in a slavish sense," says Brian Baxter of organizational development consultants Kiddy & Partners. "This is based on the realization that you can question the system without being disloyal."[32]

Today's employees are more questioning and demanding. They are confident enough to air their concerns, grievances and aspirations. If they were customers, we would call them sophisticated. It is perhaps significant that we tend not to. Maybe we should? Perhaps we must.

To handle variety, funky leaders expose themselves to more diverse experiences. Nathan Myhrvold of Microsoft also works as an assistant chef at a French restaurant in Seattle. Ole Bek of the Danish consumer electronics company Bang & Olufsen claims that he "learns much more window-shopping at Louis Vuitton in Paris than by looking at consumer electronics outlets".[33] Disney's Michael Eisner even says, "One reason we are in business with Infoseek and Starwave is to have people who will turn to us and say, 'You are so old and so stupid'."[34] To get some fresh input visit art galleries, go to rave parties, listen to opera, hang out with alcoholics or druggies, read stuff that you are not really interested in – do anything that you have never done before. Try it out – surf the Web, go skydiving, visit a museum – remember Rubbermaid.

Coming out

The great socialist project – the dream of handing over power to the people – is being realized in front of our eyes. It is being realized, not by the disciples of Communism, but by the preachers of free enterprise and market capitalism. An organization such as Manpower, the world's largest temp and talent agency, with some 600,000 individual partners, is essentially an international trade union, an employment bureau for selected global specialists. The large multinationals roaming the globe, dominating the world economy, are much the same thing – at least for those with skills scarce enough to qualify as employable.

In such a world, we have to be absolutely clear about who we are, where we want to go, and who we want to do business with, hang around with, have a relationship with and so on. If we are all condemned to freedom, we have to take control over our own lives. We can't rely on the Church, the State or any other stable institution to supply our lives with meaning any more. For us as individuals, all this implies more freedom = more opportunities = more power = more responsibility.

You be you

©Roy Lichtenstein/BUS 1999, Modern Museum, Stockholm

None of this has anything to do with politics. We are simply talking about the logical consequences of the forces of funk. It is built on insight, and insights cannot be legislated against. Tony Blair, Bill Clinton, Gerhard Schröder – none of them can do anything about it. Funky freedom is apolitical, until we pose the more critical question of if and how these forces could be put to good use in the realization of a good life. To answer this requires a new vision of the good life – a vision that actually means something to people living in the twenty-first, rather than twentieth century. Meanwhile, what is is.

In a do-it-yourself Welfare State it is all up to the individual. For better or worse, there is no one else to rely on or to blame. It is time to become head of our own head, and determinator of our own destiny. It is time to come out. The slogan of our times is UBU – you be you. The masquerade is over. Denial equals death. Successful people are successful because they are what they do and they do what they are. This begins by ridding ourselves of the roles imposed on us. We must strip down to our personality. We must ask who am I? If you dare to undress to your barest bones, you are not a mother or a father, not a manager or a subordinate, not Colored or Caucasian, not European, Asian or American. What is left? What do you really want to do with your life? The power is in your hands.

In order to thrive in this hyper-competitive environment, we need to develop a personal strategy. We need a survival kit and we need to put it together now. Good times are not around the corner unless you take a look down a lot of blind alleys.

If you aren't enjoying what you are doing – quit doing it. And quit immediately. Just listen to master investor Warren Buffett when he says, "I always worry about people who say 'I'm going to do this for ten years; I really don't like it very much. And then I'll do this ...' That's a little bit like saving sex for your old age."[35] Shopping and fucking wait for no one.

Three key things will characterize the successful funkster. These three simple traits are valid no matter what your age, gender, race, geographical origin, educational background, or occupation.

Be *unique*

Regardless of what you do, to be successful you need to be unique, at least for a moment in time. We must all strive to establish monopolies. At the same time, we have to be true to what and who we are. Nothing else will do. In a totally transparent society, we can no longer pretend to work or try to be someone else. Historically, people who were different had a hard time. Now, deviance from the norm is the recipe for survival.

It's 1976. You have $500 in your bank account and are soon to be 25. What are you going to do?

A throw one hell of a party,
B buy a used car,
C start a venture capital company investing in
   IT entrepreneurs?

Ask Ann Winblad of Hummer Winblad, one of the most successful venture capital firms in the world.

It's 1977. You have $2000 in your bank account and are soon to be 33. What are you going to do?

A party,
B car,
C start a database company?

Ask Larry Ellison, founder and CEO of Oracle.

It's 1984. You have $1000 in your bank account and are soon to be 19. What are you going to do?

A party,
B car,
C start selling PCs from your dorm room?

Ask Michael Dell.

It's 1999. What are you going to do?

The new champions will be the IWCs – idea-generators without capital – and the losers will be known as CWIs – capitalists without ideas. Talent makes capital dance.

There are basically two ways to go. First, there is the *hyper-specialist* such as Red Adair, the guy who travels around the world to put out fires in oilfields. You could become an expert

Linda Lampenius
developed
a new recipe

on a specific type of eczema, pastry, sport, musical instrument, or whatever. Focus, focus, focus and then go global. Second, you strive to be a successful *hyphenist* by combining opposites. Performance-technologists, visual-ergonomists, psycho-linguists and compu-ecologists already walk the earth. Look at Finnish centerfold-violinist Linda Lampenius, a.k.a. Linda Brava. There is a surplus of fantastic violin players worldwide. The opening up of Eastern Europe has flooded the market. Linda could be just one in the crowd. But she happens to be tall and blonde. She performs in sexy outfits, has starred in *Baywatch* and been a *Playboy* Cover Celebrity. Some of you might ask what *Playboy* and *Baywatch* have to do with playing the violin. Absolutely nothing. And that's the point. Linda is successful because she has developed a new recipe – something that did not exist prior to her arrival on the stage. Linda has a monopoly. She has invented an industry of one. Linda Brava is unique. For a moment of time Linda has made it.

Incorporate

Today, people can and do go public. Look at David Bowie. He has issued bonds on 25 albums with 300 songs – making some $60 million in doing so. Ziggy Stardust, the thin white Duke, is not alone. Doctors do it. Journalists do it. Professors do it. Programmers are doing it. We can all do it.

During the last 20 years the number of self-employed people has increased by 100 percent in the US.[36] In Europe, we see a similar trend. People are leaving their companies because their talents are either being ignored, misused or not rewarded enough in terms of cash and/or recognition. They depart to set up their own companies – Moi SA, Me plc, Jag AB, Ich Gmbh, Jeg AS, Me Inc. – business units of one. They will often continue doing the same thing, but charge twice as much, re-selling their knowledge to former employers and others.

Andy Warhol was right. However, he may have been exaggerating by around 14 and a half minutes. If we look upon our work-life as a series of gigs or projects rather than a career, constant recreation of yourself is a necessity. And you are never better than your last gig. We must look upon ourselves as a company with our own intellectual balance sheet and brand name.

We need to invest in ourselves and market ourselves. Rather than employment security, funky people go for employability – constantly updating their skills so that they are desirable to potential employers all the time and at any time.

But skills are only part of the story. Funky people also work hard to create attention and attraction. They must, because they are all players in the great global attraction game. There is a surplus of most of the skills that people embody. Incorporation is not only a question of education – investing in personal R&D. More education in itself will not solve the problem. Just look at all the MBAs or engineers. However nice the credentials, they are just faces in a very large crowd of people with similar basic training. Attraction and attention are not only a case of content, but also form. We must brand, package and market ourselves so that we are desirable. Under what slogan will you be sold?

Get connected

Nothing the slightest bit amazing has ever been done in isolation. Get ready for mingle mania. In a surplus society you are only as strong as the people you know. You may well be the smartest person in the world but if no one is aware of you it doesn't make any difference. Individual competitiveness = what you know x who you know. Overnight, each and every one of us could set up a multinational company in our garage. Using the Internet, we can reach a potential market of over 100 million people.

Focus, focus, focus, and then focus again means that we all need to find partners. We need to find partners who help us with each and every little activity and process where we are not world-class. A lot of people are used to outsourcing parts of their private lives – cleaning, daycare, etc. Now it is time to start farming out part of our working life. You need to find partners who enable you to be you. These guys are your world-class back-office, factory, marketing department, whatever. They leverage your capabilities. They allow you to come out and reach out.

Partnership power means that we will witness the emergence of dynamic clusters of expertise and knowledge. This will be fueled by greater global mobility. In the past people largely stayed where they were born or educated. Some countries

Nothing the slightest bit amazing has ever been done in isolation. Individual competitiveness = what you know x who you know.

encouraged this by not allowing you to move your assets elsewhere. Now, money and talent flows more freely.

The result will be that people will follow the leaders in their field. If countries can't close the door, they will have to provide magnets so that resources and people gravitate toward them. It is like having a party and planning who will be there. Play hip-hop and the hip-hop crowd will find their way there.

We will see the redistribution of people along tribal lines. The map of Europe and of the world will be redrawn. The United Clusters of Europe may be around the corner. Scandinavia could be home to the music cluster. Already, in India there is the Goan hippie cluster. The UK has the financial cluster in London. In the US, Vermont could be the media cluster. There is the Formula

One racing cluster in Oxfordshire and Northamptonshire, UK, the automotive cluster in Germany, the tile cluster in northern Italy. The cluster map of the world will constantly change as people move around, forming new partnerships and permutations. The important stuff – tacit knowledge – still demands a level of human interaction. You have to be breathing the same air.

Dreamanagement

We are all leaders now. We may not all be leading the ABBs and IBMs of the world, but we are all leaders. We have to be. We need to lead our own lives. Leadership is no longer something you do occasionally; it goes on every day all the time. Everything you do is leadership because you are always trying to get people to buy into what you are doing. And you are always trying to figure out who you really are. True leaders do not practice leadership – they live leadership. They are what they do.

The development of leaders has gone through three phases.[37] The first generation of business leaders were often lawyers. As the limited company was a new phenomenon, the critical knowledge required to run corporations was related to judicial matters – the legal flow. Experts were needed. Time went by. Knowledge spread. Rather than legal matters, technology became the great bean-feast. As a result, the second generation of leaders generally had an engineering background. This made sense at a time when competitive advantages came from technological innovations. Leaders managed the product flow. As time passed, new dimensions were added. Organizational and money matters became the focal point. The third generation of leaders were MBAs. They managed the financial and administrative flows.

Power exists – as it always has – in providing people with dreams.

Now everything is a question of intelligence and intangibles – knowledge flows. A great deal of critical knowledge resides in individuals. This implies that leadership is a matter of attracting and retaining great people – managing the attention flow. In turn, this means providing meaning and identity for a certain tribe. And, as leaders, we must constantly re-create this force-field of attraction and attention. It is kick-off time every day, every hour, every second. In a world where power belongs to the people, all leaders must become *humanagers*.

While a lot of people continue to believe in old-style leadership and management, they are doomed to fail. Few people admit to being lousy lovers; even fewer bosses admit to being lousy leaders. Soon, many will have to.

In organization after organization leadership is being passed on to a new type of leader. In the funky village the fuckers and shoppers have already taken over. Good or bad? It is a fact of life. The front page of *Fortune* recently trumpeted "Addicted to Sex" – corporate America's dirty little secret.[38] The cover story was a ten-page journey into the shadowlands of egomania. Freud was right: sex is all. And not only for youngsters. Just look at the leader of the free world: William Jefferson Clinton.

Little wonder then that the search for meaning is on. Look, for example, at the development of the self-help genre. Books on personal awareness abound as people try to understand themselves and their environment. The searching is an inevitable side-effect of the new world order. Our previous vision of the good life – a house, washing machine, steady job, etc. – has been undermined. Its replacement is not easily found. As a result, people shop to build an identity. Their purchases express which tribe they would like to belong to.

Power exists – as it always has – in providing people with dreams. Dreams that touch people, excite and arouse them. Once it was Marx, Kennedy and Martin Luther King who brought us dreams. Now, it is Michael Dell, Bill Gates, Anthony Robbins and Stephen Covey. In a world of diversity, a world of tribes, their dreams mean everything and nothing. The question must be how you can provide relevant and potent dreams for the tribes of the world.

feeling
funky

6

"All business is show business"

JAN CARLZON

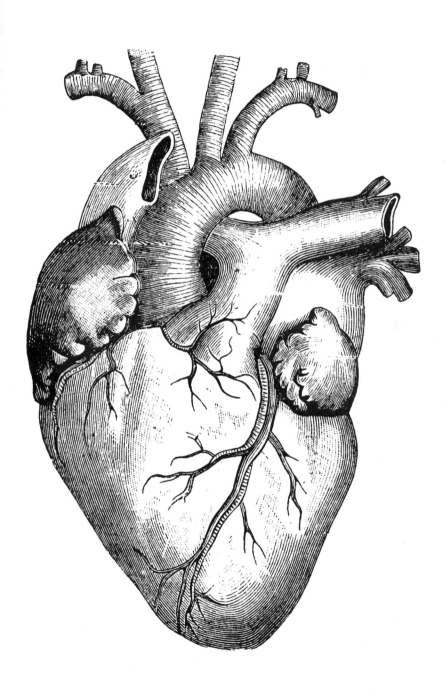

Are you ready to do business in a world with close to friction-free markets for anything from components to capital, from whale oil to engine lubricants, from perfume to alcohol? Are you ready to design, man and manage organizations that permit us to practice total innovation? Are you ready to take care of your own life, career and capabilities? Let's face it, in a knockdown Welfare State we have to build our own support systems, map out our own futures. And we have to deal with people who are motivated by anything but celibacy and savings.

That is a lot of balls to juggle in the air at the same time. Making it work is the ultimate circus act. Perhaps it is all possible. Perhaps we can catch them all as they fall towards the ground simultaneously. Perhaps we can't. The trouble is that, even if we do, it is not enough. Juggling all those balls and catching them is not enough to guarantee future success. The truth is hard to take. Juggling the balls and being able to catch them is unfortunately only a necessary, but not sufficient, condition for securing survival in a surplus society.

New balls are being continually tossed in the air. They may even be invisible. The age of abundance is slowly turning into the age of affection. Surplus must be handled not by doing more of the same but by introducing elements of sentiment and sensation. In an excess economy, the sources underlying competitiveness will gradually shift toward things that we cannot touch. Ethereal commerce. Both potential customers and prospective employees will cry out for products, services, strategies, leaders and organizations that touch them. E(motional) commerce. We all want to be touched. We crave attention. The rest is triviality.

Alberto Alessi is doing it with toilet brushes in Milan.

Richard Branson is doing it with the pensions business in the UK. Steve Jobs is doing it with computers in San Francisco. Jorma Ollila is doing it with mobile phones in Helsinki. They have all realized that we must now exploit the last taboo. The sensational society demands that we base our competitiveness on feelings and fantasy.

Making it work is the ultimate circus act

Wet dreams are made of this

Think Progressive. Think Dell. Think IKEA. Think Chevrolet Suburban. Think Stokke. Think Starbucks. And think *Legshow.* Lucrative opportunities exist everywhere. Business is not rocket science. It basically boils down to making money. Now, this may not be the reason successful companies are founded in the first place. Remember Disney and Ford setting out to respectively make people happy and democratize the automobile. For them money was just a positive result of a much greater purpose. Or, as the famous Austrian psychiatrist Victor Frankl so eloquently once put it: "For success, like happiness, cannot be pursued, it must ensue ... as the unintended side-effect of one's personal dedication to a course greater than oneself."

Greater purposes or not, all business firms need to show a profit. And in a market economy, there is but one way to make money. This explains why all managers around the world, regardless of age, gender, geographical origin and educational background, share the same wet dream. Despite all the talk about the superiority of the capitalist system and the necessity of cutthroat competition, every night, all over the globe, each and every one of these managers dreams about finding the Holy Grail of business – a temporary monopoly. And so do musicians, artists, doctors, lawyers and so on. It is the universal wet dream.

Creating temporary monopolies is exactly what managers are paid to do.

In fact, creating temporary monopolies is exactly what managers are paid to do, and often quite handsomely. Only when we are in a monopoly position can we charge prices that allow above-average profits. It may be a geographical monopoly or a product/service monopoly. If you were in the happy position of owning one, you probably wouldn't care what category it fell under.

Unfortunately, the word monopoly has had a bad press. Announcing that your core strategy is to create temporary monopolies would not be a sound business move. Customers would flee and the authorities would move in. To save you from such indignities, we suggest you refer to niches rather than monopolies – though the meaning is exactly the same.

By focusing on a specific tribe – a geographical market or certain customers – we hope to avoid competition and price wars. We want to be the only natural "choice" for our target customers, by leaving them with no choice. To be a successful niche competitor you need to be different. Funky firms follow the advice of the computer company Apple: they think different – then they rethink it again. We all want products or services that are unique in some respect – offerings that capture the attention of a specific tribe.

Basically, there are only two ways in which you can be different – either you are perceived as cheaper or you are perceived as better. But uniqueness is not only a question of the customer offering as such. There is nothing particularly original about the *products* of a company such as Dell. Uniqueness can come from anything – an idea, the business logic, the packaging, the culture or the people.

Being different is the key. That's why firms are so dependent on people who can come up with unique ideas. The trouble is that uniqueness and difference are often the preserve of people who, judged against the average corporate citizen, are a little strange, not to say weird. **Normality is the route to nowhere.** These are the true entrepreneurs, people prepared to challenge the status quo, to look at the world with totally open eyes, break the rules, ignore regulations, and question the norms. They are prepared to take risks, personal risks. The question must be whether or not we are willing to take risks. Would you and your organization take risks in the quest for temporary monopolies?

Of course, there is only one answer because there is no longer any choice. Normality is the route to nowhere. If we are only willing to behave like all the others, we will see the same things, hear the same things, hire similar people, come up with similar ideas, and develop identical products or services. We will drown in the sea of normality. And Normal Inc. is bankrupt.

Abnormality creates monopolies – our 15 minutes of capitalist fame. And, if weirdness is the only way to wealth, think again about the weird-factor at your organization. Is it really high enough? Opportunities are just waiting to be discovered, but we have to look at unexplored places – places where our competitors have not already been 343 times. Otherwise we are doomed to see what all the others have already seen. Monopolists make money.

From location to organization

If you don't believe us, consider the evolution of competitiveness. In the beginning, competitive advantage was primarily derived from location. Access to various raw materials provided the firm-specific advantages necessary to create and exploit temporary monopolies. The successful company of the nineteenth century profited from access to oil, forests, mines, etc., and made families, such as the Rockefellers and the Gettys, incredibly rich. It was a question of finding and exploiting the Klondikes of the world.

Advantage location

But the capitalist economy is ruthless. Soon, free markets for raw materials made it increasingly difficult to use location as the single source of competitive advantage. As this happened, innovation and technology, combined with access to capital, became the new differentiators. The key to competitiveness was creating more value out of the same input. As a result, at the turn of the twentieth century, the business community was dominated by a few capitalists and a number of innovatory entrepreneurs – people like the Wallenbergs, Thomas Alva Edison, J.P. Morgan, Alfred Nobel, the Rothschilds, and Otto Diesel. Competitive edge was based on ingenuity.

Once again the market struck back. Products were imitated and patents were sold or acquired. When these innovations were turned into everyone's property, competitive advantage could no longer be based on a now-defunct technological monopoly.

We then entered the organizational age. Pioneers such as Alfred P. Sloan and Henry DuPont in the US designed the multidivisional firm – splitting up the company into smaller, product-focused units. The new organization allowed a continuous upgrading of previous technological advantages. This organizational innovation became the dominant model for most large and complex US firms, allowing them to conquer the world. It made sense given that all firms exploited similar technologies. The ones with superior organizational solutions succeeded. Later, European firms adopted the model and the international competitive playing field was forced to the horizontal.

Advantage innovation

Progressively, throughout the latter half of the twentieth century, a plethora of organizational innovations have given rise to minor and major temporary monopolies. Just in time (JIT), business process re-engineering (BPR), management by objectives (MBO), total quality management (TQM), management by walking around (MBWA), *Kanban*, benchmarking, matrix management, outsourcing, downsizing, strategic alliances, and lean production – the list could go on *ad infinitum* – have all created a glimmer of competitive advantage for those who were first to fully capitalize on them. For most, as always, the glimmer was a distant and fleeting glimpse.

The organization has moved on. Gone (theoretically, at least) is the bureaucratic firm described by Max Weber almost a century ago. Right now, if you belong to the organizational in-crowd, your firm is supposed to look like a blueberry pancake, a fishnet, a shamrock, gazelles, or even boiling spaghetti (according to Oticon). Most modern firms still base their competitiveness on developing an organizational solution that enables them to uphold a fruitful balance between exploiting givens and creating novelty.

In a world of surpluses, novelty is usually in short supply. Companies, managers and human beings have a lemming-like capacity to follow each other. Sameness is infectious. In search of

Advantage organization

organizational inspiration, companies turn to global consulting companies. They see a competitor that has re-engineered, so they hire a consultant to design a re-engineering program for them. The dominoes fall. Soon most companies in an industry have been re-engineered. The consulting firms are better off. But, there is little in the way of competitive advantage to be extracted from doing something everyone else has already done. Andersen Consulting, McKinsey & Company, Boston Consulting Group and Cap Gemini, to name but a few, all contribute to the current homogenization of organizational solutions around the world.

Not only that. Think about all the MBA students and those people who get a masters degree in science. Every year they invade companies around the world. As competent as they may be, they belong to a group of globally standardized individuals. Whether you go to a business or engineering school in Moscow or Manila, Seattle or San Sebastian does not really matter. You are exposed to the same models, books and formulas. These students are then let loose, equipped with identical recipes for how to succeed.

As virtually all firms become wired, IT will act as a homogenizing force, making company organizations ever more similar.

Similarly, the introduction of information technology has given certain companies initial advantages. But, as virtually all firms become wired, IT will act as a homogenizing force, making company organizations ever more similar. Technology tends to have that effect. Just think of what has happened to cars after the introduction of wind tunnels and CAD/CAM. When we were young, and our parents took us out for a drive, we competed with our younger brothers trying to guess the brands of the cars that passed us. Today, who can tell the difference?

Sameness is a fact. Ericsson must have world-class, state-of-the-art technology. It must pioneer new organizational solutions. The firm needs the best IT solutions that money can buy. Ericsson must attract, recruit and retain the top people on the job market. It must work with the best suppliers in the world, not the closest. All this is necessary. There is no choice. But, it is not sufficient because Nokia is also doing it. Philips is doing it. Motorola is doing it. Sony is doing it. Siemens is doing it. They are all doing it.

The consequence is that competitiveness can no longer be solely based on location, technological innovation, or organization. Any advantages these might provide are likely to be extremely short-lived. Instead, true competitiveness must be built around something we all know exists but which is seldom discussed in business situations. Companies must base their temporary monopolies on emotions and imagination. E-competitiveness.

Economies of soul

Exploiting the last taboo means departing from the tradition that people are to be treated as just another factor of production – a human resource or an anonymous consumer. People do not enjoy being treated as human resources or as a nameless and faceless customer X; they want to be seen and recognized as individuals. We have to tap the hidden treasures of the extended organizational tribe and its members. We have to start competing on the basis of feelings and fantasy – emotion and imagination.

Most individuals, consumers as well as colleagues, already are, or at least could be, driven by a rationale that extends far beyond the purely economic one. As Alberto Alessi, founder of the company with the same name, once said, "People have an enormous need for art and poetry that industry does not yet understand."[1] As Alessi charges some $80 for a toilet brush, he must be doing something right.

People have an enormous need for art and poetry that industry does not yet understand

There is money in emotion. This is not an obscure flaky agenda. It may represent the antithesis to the previous commercial rationale but it is not anti-commercialism. It is the new commercialism. It is not flaky – it is funky. Poetry and profits need not be mutually exclusive. If contemporary business was only a case of bits, brains and brands – why does Citibank work with Elton John? Why did Motorola and Microsoft team up with the Rolling Stones? And why did Miller enter an alliance with MC Hammer? The answer is short and melodic: vibes.

Even traditional industrial firms admit that emotion and imagination are the way forward. Just listen to one of the head designers at Ford:

"In the past we tended to focus inwardly, looking for functional efficiency. Now the mindshift is to more outwardly focused, emotional satisfaction for the consumer."[2] It makes you wonder what old Henry would have said. Our guess would be that if it lowered costs and boosted sales, Henry would have grasped the concept immediately. Capitalists turn into humanists the instant this metamorphosis proves profitable.

The reality is that the company that aspires to be competitive cannot deprive itself of the strengths associated with what we call "economies of soul".

Soul is heartfelt, personal, sexual. It touches us. Not everyone wants to be touched – especially when they buy a toilet brush.

Vibes, vibes, vibes

While the best (and worst) things in life are associated with strong feelings, if you mention words like love, lust, glad, wild, or zany in most corporate settings, people rush from the room. Some four-letter words always offend.

Forget causing offence. IQ and EQ must co-exist. In an excess economy, success comes from attracting the emotional consumer or colleague – not the rational one. But, in a day and age when you really need to know these people by heart, many executives don't even seem to know them by name.

Cold, dead fish

As for our customers, economies of soul mean focusing on the extended experience, trying to look and think beyond the atoms or bits. As someone once remarked, sushi is really cold, dead fish, but that isn't what the customer buys or how it should be marketed. Then, why do so many companies still persist in selling cold, dead fish to consumers who are much more interested in sushi?

What is a woman purchasing lipstick really buying? Well, at one level, it is colored fat in a plastic container. But, at another level, she is really buying hope, the hope that someone will tell her "You are so beautiful, I love you, let's go to my place". That is, at least, what most men buy when they go shopping for after-shave and we can't really see why there should be any difference. This reasoning applies to all products. What do we really buy when we come home with a Nokia mobile phone, a pair of Gap khakis, or a Sony Walkman?

The moral: what companies sell and what their customers buy are two different things. Therefore, every once in a while it is wise to place yourself in the shoes of your customers and ask the question: "What are they really buying?" The answer, 99 times out of 100, is not what you think you are selling.

Economies of soul are also concerned with our colleagues. We need to understand what makes them mad, sad, and glad, as Manfred Kets de Vries of INSEAD puts it. We need to become masters of playing the emotional strings on our own and their lyres. How can we expect to motivate and inspire people when we have not got a clue about what makes them tick? We should all learn something from Herb Kelleher at SouthWest Airlines. "We are not afraid to talk to our people with emotions. We're not afraid to tell them, 'We love you' because we do," says Kelleher.[3]

And profiting from soul economies begins with understanding ourselves. What really makes you mad, sad, and glad? Just look at Bill Gates – his nerdship. Mr Gates created his (temporary?) monopoly by getting the Microsoft operating system into all IBM computers throughout the world. Right now, he is the richest person on planet Earth. Yet we are sure that it is not money that drives Bill Gates. Money is merely a positive side-effect.

In fact, we should all know what drives Bill because we have all met him – at least three times. The first time was in kindergarten. Bill was the tiny boy sitting outside the sandbox. Every now and then, the tough guys turned around and threw sand in his eyes. The second time was in third grade. It was gym class and time to play soccer. Bill Gates was the tiny guy, now with glasses, who got picked last – after the girls. The third time we met him was at prom night. Bill was the skinny and badly dressed guy, now with really thick glasses, standing in the corner eating snacks and drinking soda. He came alone, and none of the girls wanted to dance with him. Do you remember him now?

Mad, sad, glad

What makes Bill Gates mad, sad, and glad? What makes him tick? It might be – revenge. Revenge against all the kids who threw sand in his eyes, all those who neglected to pick him when it was time to play soccer, and all the girls who refused to dance with him at prom night. And if you belong to one of those groups you'd better beware, because Bill's back and this time he's in charge. Microsoft is the vehicle – revenge is the fuel. Get mad. Get even. Get happy.

Infinite innovation

Conventional levels of and perspectives on innovation will get us nowhere. Economies of soul do not emerge from predictable, incremental innovation. To be successful in the twenty-first century we will have to learn how to practice infinite innovation. Infinite innovation is the never-ending pursuit of creating more and more value for all stakeholders inside and outside the organization. Infinite = endless. Or as Chris Bangle, head of design at BMW, expresses it, "It's a matter of do, do, do – Max DoDo."

But infinite innovation also requires that we focus on the infinite aspects of what we offer prospective customers and colleagues. Infinite = limitless. Both time and space, for instance, are finite dimensions – races with finishing lines. Even if you come first, after reaching the finishing line, there is nothing more to do other than hang around waiting for the competitors to arrive. Innovation may be instant and international, but it does not carry infinite opportunities. There is nothing beyond real time and everywhere. What made Nike or Starbucks coffeeshops so successful? Well, it wasn't simply their speed or their global reach.

This does not mean that we advise organizations to go back to being slow and local. It is simply that it is hard to see how you can build *sustainable* competitive advantages in finite dimensions. What is a novelty today is bound to become a commodity next week or even tomorrow. Even worse, every time we make a move, we are also moving closer and closer to the real-time, global wall. Again, doing well in these aspects is necessary but not sufficient.

Think about when you last bought a PC. What were the sales arguments – price, performance, gigabytes, and megahertz? Well, in a true excess economy, all those are given. From a strict price/performance view it will not really matter which vacuum cleaner, TV set, VCR, or microwave the customer buys. They are all more or less equally good. Remember what J.D. Power said about cars, "Today, there are no bad cars." Getting that stuff right only buys you a ticket to take part in the game. If you and your company cannot fix the basics you are part of the crowd.

Finite dimensions also happen to be objectively measurable and clear. As a result, it is easy for consumers to evaluate the performance of different competitors. Add to this the enabling effect of the Net. Spray, Yahoo and CompareNet are not only portals or search engines. They are compare engines. Finite strategies + the Net mean that comparison-shopping becomes a piece of cake for the well-informed customer. By focusing on these finite aspects of the offering, companies enable the customer to be even more demanding. Consequently, in this rational world, there is also a clear risk (or chance) that the winner will take all. Are you willing to take that bet?

Infinite dimensions, however, allow us to escape from the fate of always being at the mercy of the demanding customer. By focusing on implementing our competitive advantages in infinite dimensions, we make sure that there is no end to our endeavors. A customer offering can always become more stylish, attractive or sensational; there is no end to how friendly we can behave in relation to our customers and colleagues; there is no limit to how creative an organization can become.

Business just isn't a finite game – never has been and never will be. Even Bill Gates admits that, "You will never go to a Microsoft meeting and hear somebody say, 'let's win' or 'we won' because that has a finite scale to it."[4]

Moreover, infinite dimensions are open to subjective interpretations. What captures our attention may not capture yours, and vice versa. People differ in terms of what they like and dislike. Funk = diversity. Remember that for the typical masochist heaven is hell. Infinite innovation provides us with the dimensions needed to target the interests of specific tribes. Naturally, this also means saying no to certain customers. Not all people like the design of Helmut Lang's clothes or Alessi's kettles. A lot of people genuinely disliked the Benetton ads featuring AIDS patients and pictures of war casualties from the Balkans. This was not harmful to Benetton. Indeed, it wanted a reaction. Its judgment was that its potential market would be intrigued, impressed or have different positive responses to its ads.

It is better to be something for someone than nothing to everyone. The danger of focusing on finite dimensions is that you may well end up as nothing to anyone.

In an emotional economy, it is better to piss off 90 percent of the people while capturing the attention and interest of the other 10 percent, than to be merely OK to all of them. Since the early 1990s, some CDs have carried stickers with parental warnings that they contain explicit lyrics. Why not have this for all customer offerings? Explicit design. Explicit content. Being banned pays. Some customers become glad, others sad or mad. But at least they feel something. They are not ignorant. Why don't we have X-rated jeans, X-rated cars or X-rated vacuum cleaners?

In an emotional economy, it is better to piss off 90 percent of the people.

This reasoning applies to all products and services in all countries. In the new world, OK, average and almost, won't do. People want amazing things, spectacular things, funky things. The new economy is more like figure skating than speed skating – you score points for artistic impression (and you do need to get into the mind of the Ukranian judge).

Sensational strategies

To profit from infinite innovation, we need to focus our energy on a few of these more elusive dimensions. Competitive strategy is the route to nowhere. We need to create sensational strategies. Sensational strategies capture the attention of the people with whom we want to do business. Sensational strategies appeal to all five senses of man. They embrace our emotions. Competitive strategy means being one step ahead. Sensational strategy is about playing a different game.

The first sensational strategy is concerned with ethics. Today's journalists are expert at finding skeletons in our closets. In a

CNN village, global gossip travels at the speed of light. Total transparency will undress the unscrupulous. People and organizations that do not understand this may mean they find themselves removed from the hall of fame to the hall of shame. And, in this way at least, a market economy is deeply democratic. Customers vote with their money; one dollar one vote. Competents vote with their minds; one idea one vote. No capitalism without representation. If you use child labor or don't care about the environment, customers will take their business elsewhere. And, so too, will most investors and intellectuals. Few people want to work for and invest in toxic companies, as Stanford's Jeffrey Pfeffer prefers to call them.

All things being equal, the caring capitalist will always beat the evil enterprise. The Body Shop's Anita Roddick created a temporary monopoly from the simple idea that there was a market for cosmetics that had not been tested on animals and which only contained natural ingredients. Companies increasingly want to appear caring. For example, the automotive company Toyota is currently developing trees that absorb toxic gases.[5] Caring needs to be accompanied by credibility. Funky organizations have total ethics. Ethics must concern everyone and everything at a firm. They must be practiced everywhere, continually. You just cannot be a little ethical or merely ethical when it suits you. Ethics is absolute.

OWW4 meets PWE: Organizations Worth Working For meets People Worth Employing.

In an age of affection and abundance, ethics is also a potent competitive weapon. It can provide a means of differentiation – rarely has it already been fully exploited by the competition. We can use ethics to attract new customers *and* employees. Today it's OWW4 meets PWE: Organizations Worth Working For meets People Worth Employing. As a company, you get the employees you deserve and vice versa. Do not expect anything else. From this perspective, a firm works very much like a fish. It rots from the head down. If the top of the organization does not provide good role models, why should the rest of the organization behave like good citizens?

The second sensational strategy focuses on aesthetics. From the global dispersion of technologies and skills it follows that most products and services are similar. So, if the interior is more or less the same, we must start competing through the exterior appearance of our products and services. Contemplate these words of wisdom from renowned designer Philippe Starck: "People take technology for granted these days. What they want are warm, friendly products – something to seduce them."[6] So come on, amaze us, daze us, and seduce us.

We can see this throughout the business world. Companies such as Philips and Bosch sell their mobile phones through their design. Swedish retailer H&M used to be known as a copycat in the fashion industry. Now, it has 60 in-house designers. Nike goes one step further and employs 350 designers. Is your company design-driven? BMW's Chris Bangle, says: "Design is meaning." If your company is not interested in design, it is meaningless. Everything has a form. If it has a form, it has a meaning. You have to have a design. As Chris Bangle observes, it is impossible not to have a form. But design is not only form. Design also equals functionality, costs, lifestyle and lifespan.

Design is about truth, love and beauty – and, increasingly, about whether a business has a sensational strategy or the same strategy as everyone else. In this design-driven world, everything is a fashion accessory. There is fashion in everything – the beautiful train, the trendy wrench and the stylish lawnmower. A good price/performance relationship is necessary but no longer sufficient. One of us visited a computer games company in Silicon Valley where games are developed and launched in winter and summer collections. Fashion rules – and the only fashion victims are those who fail to keep pace. Again, this is not only a case of the limited customer offering. Aesthetics concerns all aspects of the organization and in how we deal with customers and colleagues – the office architecture, the stores, packaging, salespeople and so on.

Brands and marketing communication are part of this extended aesthetic experience. In a surplus society, in which people are condemned to freedom, brands reduce uncertainty. They enable us to communicate who we are, or maybe who we would like to be. Brands implicitly convey trust and recognition. Anything can be branded. Even products that most of us never see – look at Intel. Brands make us feel safe. You are in Tokyo. Cultural mega-shock. People everywhere. Uncertainty fever. To soothe your weary head you put on your Levi's jeans, Calvin Klein shirt and Nike sneakers. You leave the Sheraton hotel and head for McDonald's to enjoy a McFeast burger and a Coke. Brands are valium for our souls – lighthouses in a chaotic world. How else can we explain the fact that 150 million Unilever products are sold every day and that 1.2 billion people daily use Gillette products.[7] What you ask for is what you get. Zero-variance. Only foreseeable surprises. No wonder the Coca-Cola brand is worth some $50 billion. The Coca-Cola company could probably burn down all its physical assets and still go to the bank the next day to borrow a couple of $100 million. How much could you borrow? Burn it down – build something sensational.

Building the emotional enterprise

So, how do we unleash the potential for emotional competitiveness and corporate imagination? At least in the West, the preferred approach for handling increased organizational complexity or new organizational dimensions has been to add yet another box to the organizational chart. Somewhere in the world we are sure a manager will read this book and, as a result, set up a department for emotions and imagination. They may – to finish the job properly – appoint a male, 46.5-year-old to run the unit. Ridiculous? We hope so, but it closely resembles the way in which we have gone about handling issues such as quality and knowledge during the last 20 years. Stripping people of their freedom is not the proper response to funk.

It is ridiculous and, what's more, it doesn't work. Think of the firms that created strategic planning departments in the 1960s. Did they plan the future successfully? Did they, for example, anticipate the oil crisis of the early 1970s? Did they foresee the fall of the Berlin Wall? Professor James

Emotion and imagination is not a department, it is a philosophy, an attitude.

Brian Quinn goes as far as to say that the process of strategic planning is like a ritual raindance. The main objective is not to make it rain, however, but to become better dancers. Consider all the companies that set up quality departments in the 1980s. How many quality organizations can you see? There are thousands of customer service departments, yet customer service is as bad as always.

Not that long ago we did some consulting for a major department store in Sweden. The company had experienced tremendous problems with shoplifting. Finally, management decided to do something. They appointed a head of security to take care of the problem. The result: more things disappeared. The reason: by making this issue a big thing for a select few, the others stopped caring.

Message: the critical components and true sources of competitive advantage, such as knowledge, quality and people stuff must be turned into a small thing for all people in the organization. Funky organizations have already realized that emotion and imagination is not a department, it is a philosophy, an attitude. But they do not turn this philosophy into organizational action by merely reasoning with people – they have already moved far beyond that.

Reason — Head

Affection — Heart

Intuition — Gut

Desire — Groin

There are basically four ways in which you can communicate with people no matter who they are: either you appeal to their Reason, Affection, Intuition or their Desire. Whereas reason is a question of logic, affection concerns love, intuition is about second sight, and desire equals lust. Every time we communicate with someone we use a mix of R, A, I and D. Just take the latest slogan created by your organization – a new mission statement or an ad – and rank it in terms of the four dimensions.

But the critical question is whether or not you are using a potent mix. In an age of abundance and information overload, where attention is a scarce resource, are you really getting through? Are you striking the right keys? Is something lacking? We suspect that most organizations and individuals could load their message with more feelings. Instead of just reasoning with people

240

it is time to start AID-ing them – appealing to their affection, intuition and desire.

Most managers are experts in the first category – lawyers, engineers and MBAs alike. This is where they got their training and experience – they are playing a logic game. Reasoning is what the typical manager is rewarded for. Eventually the analytical side of the brain grows so large and heavy that some executives find it difficult to avoid walking in circles.

The problem is that in an age of affection, success depends less and less on our reasoning skills. There are millions of super-smart, IQ-packed people out there. In the new economy, it is your task to bring people on a journey into an uncertain and chaotic future – every day. As Professor Noel Tichy of the University of Michigan says, "The best way to get people to venture into unknown terrain is to make it desirable by taking them there in their imagination."[8]

Doing so requires that we exploit the A, the I and the D – rather than going nowhere with rational reasoning. Stories and storytelling are about AID-ing.

Success requires that you lower the aim from the head to the rest of the body.

Spinning people does not imply more reasoning. "You've got to evangelize the concept," says John Chambers, CEO of Cisco Systems.[9]

The only way to create real profit is to attract the emotional rather than rational consumer and colleague by appealing to their feelings and fantasy. If you try reasoning, you will have to deal with the purely economic rationality of the demanding customer or calculating co-worker. This inevitably results in zero profits as you will compete globally with an infinite number of other similar firms. And, from an internal perspective, the best possible result is competence without commitment – the first step in performing competence castration surgery. Instead, success requires that you lower the aim from the head to the rest of the body.

The way to trick the trap of the market is to refocus from the head to the heart, gut and groin of people – to go after their affection, intuition and desire. Let's say you are throwing a party for your closest friends. What will determine whether or not this is to be the best party of their lives? The product: good food and a decent bottle(s) of wine will obviously help. But at least one or two of your friends could probably outperform you by turning to an even better caterer or wine store. Again the product as such is given – necessary but not sufficient. What will matter is whom you invite and how good you are at creating an attractive atmosphere.

Look at the return of music festivals. At such happenings, the audiences – the customers – are the real stars. Success and large crowds rests with turning fans into stars. Berlin is made attractive through the annual Love Parade, and in Stockholm there's the Water Festival. All cities have buildings. All cities have roads and parks. Atoms abound. It is the soft stuff that really matters. Cities also take part in the great global attraction game. And so do you. What is your organization currently doing to make the customers feel like stars?

Involving the customers sometimes just happens. The hapless English cricket team is now followed by a "Barmy Army". This collection of vocal supporters has traveled the world following the team. Cheap air travel now makes this possible for a growing number of people – when England played in the West Indies there were 10,000 English supporters. Not content with following the team, the Barmy Army is now turning into a business, selling T-shirts and memorabilia. The followers have become the news story and a decidedly tribal business.

The same reasoning is valid in most business situations. Just look at Harley-Davidson. The company and the customer offering are not for everyone. You have to share some traits with the other members of the Harley tribe. The company is not just selling a motorcycle; it is selling American nostalgia. The arguments for buying a Harley have little to do with rational reasoning – price or performance – and everything to do with affection, intuition and desire. CEO Richard Teerlink agrees by saying, "There's a high degree of emotion that drives our success. We symbolize the feelings of freedom and independence that people really want in this stressful world."[10]

Or look at the Apple team that developed the first Mac. They believed their computer would not only change computing, but the whole world. The team had a soul. The members were driven by the desire to make a difference. When Steve Jobs was trying to recruit John Sculley from Pepsi, he just asked him, "Do you want to spend the rest of your life selling sugared water, or do you want a chance to change the world?"[11] Sculley took his chance.

It is time to start treating customers and critical competents as celebrity guests. These people show up when they want to, and they will leave when they feel like it. To keep them happy, we can't just sit back and do nothing. There is no way we can talk them into staying. We have got to prove our commitment in action by entertaining them – keeping them happy. We have to create *emotional switching costs*. Building a true tribe means instituting the same kinds of relationships that (used to?) exist in a family. Breakups, divorces and unexpected deaths or lost customers and defecting employees should result in a lot of anxiety – on both sides.

Emotional switching costs

If you think this sounds excessive then listen to Ken Alvares, head of worldwide human resources at Sun Microsystems. He says that the goal "is to keep people so busy having fun everyday that they don't even listen when the headhunters call".[12] We all know that happy people do a better job, but how many companies have words such as fun and happiness included in their vision or mission statements? Remember that a pretty good predictor of a company's performance is the average number of laughs per employee per day.

The average never wins

In an age of affection, all organizations compete with each other. The industries, regions and markets they are active in no longer really matter. Competition is not specific and centered on providing great jobs or products, excellent services or career opportunities. In the emotional economy, competition is generic and revolves around who can provide people, consumers and co-workers with a good life. It is about providing people with dreams. And the definition of what this life really means will differ from tribe to tribe, person to person, and from time to time. The important thing is that we are in charge.

There is no doubt that we are going to see tremendous wealth-creation in the years to come. The trillion-dollar question is who is going to share this wealth? Of one thing we can be sure: the average never wins. It never has and never will. What is different in the age of abundance is that the average is currently getting an additional three billion new individual members, an uncountable number of new companies, and a plethora of new products and services. Even so, looking forward ten years, your greatest competitors are probably still unborn and unknown. And, all these individuals and organizations want to share the new wealth – they want a piece of the cake.

To succeed, we must stop being so goddamn normal. If we behave like all the others, we will see the same things, come up with similar ideas, and develop identical products or services. At its best, normal output will produce normal results. In a winner takes all world, normal = nothing. But, if we are willing to take one little risk, break one tiny rule, disregard a few of the norms, there is at least a theoretical chance that we will come up with something different, actually get a niche, create a short-term monopoly and make a little money.

Funky business is like playing the lottery. If you participate, there is a 99 percent chance that you will lose. On the other hand, if you do not take part, your chances of losing are 100 percent.

To succeed we have to go for that single percent. The future belongs to the outliers – those who dare to take risks, break rules and make new ones. The future belongs to those who seize the opportunity to create it.

So, if we are indeed living in a surplus society, an emotional economy, on the verge of friction-free capitalism, what can we do? Well, the answer is quite simple. Our only chance of surviving and thriving in this crazy world is to excel in exploiting the last taboo.

People expect good stuff. They have become used to great value for money. And they can get that from almost all companies around the world. So, being great is no longer good enough. Customer satisfaction is not enough. To succeed we have to surprise people. We have to attract and addict them. Attention is all. By focusing only on the hardcore aspects of business we risk becoming irrelevant. And trust us, irrelevancy is a much greater problem that inefficiency. The only thing more difficult than learning to exploit the last taboo of emotion and imagination is learning to thrive without it. So, people and organizations of the world – come out. Or you will be carried out.

NOTES

Foreword

1   This is an actual quote from a Public Goverment Report SOU 1998:65 (translated into English).

1 Funky times

1   *Financial Times,* November 7/8, 1998.

2   American psychologist Karl Lashley conducted these experiments on rats. As long as the visual cortex is kept intact, a rat can still find its way through a maze. We genuinely dislike such experiments but what is is. Consult Taylor, G. R., *The Natural History of the Mind,* Dutton, New York, 1979, for a more detailed discussion.

3   *The Economist,* September 28, 1996.

4   Crainer, S., *Business the Jack Welch Way,* AMACOM, New York, 1999.

5   Wayne Calloway, late CEO of Pepsi, in a speech to the MBA students at Harvard Business School, Boston, Massachusetts, 1992.

6   Stewart, T. A., *Intellectual Capital: The new wealth of organizations,* Doubleday/Currency New York, 1997.

7   *Time* magazine, Millennium issue.

8   Stewart, T. A., *Intellectual Capital: The new wealth of organizations,* Doubleday/Currency, New York, 1997.

9   Negroponte, N., *Being Digital.* Alfred A. Knopf, New York, 1995.

10   Hymer, S., *The International Operations of National Firms: A study of direct investment,* Unpublished dissertation, MIT, Massachusetts, 1960.

11   See Johansson, J. & Vahlne, J-E., "The Internationalization Process of the Firm: A model of knowledge development and increasing market commitment", *Journal of International Business Studies,* Vol. 8, 1977 for the original theoretical argument. Also see Nordström, K. A., *The Internationalization Process of the Firm: Searching for new patterns and explanations,* IIB, Stockholm, 1991 for some more recent results.

12   Micklewait, J. & Wooldridge, A., *The Witch Doctors: Making sense of the management gurus,* Times Books Random House, New York, 1996.

13   Ibid.

14   *Fortune,* March 15, 1999.

15   *Time,* April 13, 1998.

16   Knoke, W., *Bold New World: The essential road map to the twenty-first century,* Kodansha International, 1996.

17   *Fortune,* September 5, 1994.

18   *The Economist,* March 29, 1997.

19   Cairncross, F., *The Death of Distance: How the communications revolution will change our lives,* Orion, London, 1997.

20   *Fortune,* September 5, 1994.

21   *Financial Times Handbook of Management,* FT/Pitman, London, 1995.

22 Ibid.

23 *The Economist*, September 28, 1996.

24 Haag, M. & Pettersson, B., *Percy Barnevik: Makten, myten, människan*, Ekelids Förlag, 1998.

25 Peters, T., *Liberation Management*, Alfred A. Knopf, New York, 1992.

26 Crainer, S., *The Ultimate Book of Business Quotations*, AMACOM, New York, 1998.

27 The examples are borrowed from Tapscott, D., *The Digital Economy: Promise and peril in the age of networked intelligence*, McGraw-Hill, New York, 1996.

28 Davies, S. & Meyer, C., *Blur: The speed of change in the connected economy*, Capstone, Oxford, 1998.

29 All figures in the examples are borrowed from Taylor, J. & Wacker, W. (with Means, H.), *The 500 Year Delta: What happens after what comes next*, Harper Business, London, 1997.

30 This argument was originally made by Taylor, J. & Wacker, W. (with Means, H.), *The 500 Year Delta: What happens after what comes next,* Harper Business, London, 1997.

31 *Fortune*, June 23, 1997.

32 Finley, M., *Technocrazed: The businessperson's guide to controlling technology– before it controls you*, Peterson's/Pacesetter Books, Princeton, New Jersey, 1995.

2 Forces of funk

1 *Financial Times*, March 15, 1999.

2 *Fortune*, March 1, 1999.

3 Stewart, T. A., *Intellectual Capital: The new wealth of organizations*, Doubleday/Currency, New York, 1997.

4 *Finanstidningen*, October 3–5, 1998.

5 Toffler, A., *The Third Wave*, Bantam, New York, 1980.

6 Davies, S. & Davidson, B., 2020 *Vision: Transform your business today to succeed in tomorrow's economy*, Simon & Schuster, New York, 1991.

7 Tapscott, D., *The Digital Economy: Promise and peril in the age of networked intelligence*, McGraw-Hill, New York, 1996.

8 Negroponte, N., *Being Digital*. Alfred A. Knopf, New York, 1995.

9 Moore's Law states that the cost of computing power halves every 18 months.

10 *Wired*, October, 1998.

11 Tapscott, D., *The Digital Economy: Promise and peril in the age of networked intelligence*, McGraw-Hill, New York, 1996.

12 For a deeper discussion, see Hagel III, J. & Singer, M., *Net Worth: Shaping markets when customers make the rules*, Harvard Business School Press, Boston, Massachusetts, 1999.

13 Tapscott, D., *The Digital Economy: Promise and peril in the age of networked intelligence*, McGraw-Hill, New York, 1996.

14 *Business Week*, March 22, 1999.

15 Tapscott, D., *The Digital Economy: Promise and peril in the age of networked intelligence*, McGraw-Hill, New York, 1996.

16 *Business Week*, October 16, 1995.

17 Ibid.

18 *Wired*, May, 1998.

19 Marshall, A., *Principles of Economics*, 2nd ed., 1890, Reprinted London, Macmillan, 1920.

20 *Wired*, April, 1998.

21 In reality, most of the business schools were founded during the 1960s.

22 Ohmae, Kenichi, *Triad Power*, Free Press, New York, 1985.

23 Pascale, Richard, Athos, Anthony, & Goss, Tracy, "The reinvention roller coaster", *Harvard Business Review*, November–December, 1993.

24 de Geus, A., *The Living Company*, Harvard Business School Press, Boston, Massachusetts, 1997.

25 Taylor, J. & Wacker, W. (with Means, H.), *The 500 Year Delta: What happens after what comes next*, Harper Business, London, 1997.

26 *Fortune*, March 20, 1995.

27 Guitton, S., *The Pope Speaks*, Meredith Press, 1968.

3 Funky village

1   Geelmuyden & Kiese A/S, internal research material, 1997.

2   *Fast Company*, December, 1998.

3   *Wired*, March, 1999.

4   Fradette, M. & Michaud, S., *The Power of Corporate Kinetics: Create the self-adapting, self-renewing instant-action enterprise*, Simon & Schuster, New York, 1998.

5   Ibid.

6   Tapscott, D., *The Digital Economy: Promise and peril in the age of networked intelligence*, McGraw-Hill, New York, 1996.

7   *Fortune*, October 27, 1997.

8   *Fortune*, March 11, 1996.

9   Mulgan, G., *Connexity: How to live in a connected world*, Harvard Business School Press, Boston, Massachusetts, 1997.

10 Ibid.

11 *Business Week*, February 16, 1998.

12 Ghoshal, S. & Bartlett, C., in *Financial Times Handbook of Management*, FT/Pitman, London, 1995.

13 Cairncross, F., *The Death of Distance: How the communications revolution will change our lives*, Orion, London, 1997.

14 Taylor, J. & Wacker, W. (with Means, H.), *The 500 Year Delta: What happens after what comes next*, Harper Business, London, 1997.

15 *Business Week*, March 22, 1999.

16 *Fortune*, December 7, 1998.

17 *Fast Company*, January, 1999.

18 *Fast Company*, April–May, 1998.

19 A similar idea is developed by Davies, S. & Meyer, C., in *Blur: The speed of change in the connected economy*, Capstone, Oxford, 1998.

20 Jager, R. M. & Ortiz, R., *In the Company of Giants: Candid conversations with the visionaries of the digital world*, McGraw-Hill, New York, 1997.

21 *Wired*, May, 1998.

22 *The World in 1999*, The Economist Publications, London, 1999.

23 *Fast Company*, February–March, 1999.

24 *The Economist*, May 31, 1997.

25 *Fortune*, December 8, 1998.

26 *Air Transport World*, October, 1996.

27 *Financial Times*, January 11, 1998.

28 Crainer, S., *The Freethinker's A–Z*, Capstone, Oxford, 1999.

29 Kelly, S., "Information is the fuel of a new industrial revolution", *Data Warehousing 98,* November 1998.

30 *Fortune*, November 10, 1997.

31 *Financial Times*, December 8, 1998. The figures for 1990 are at May 31 (*Business Weekly*), and the figures for 1998 are at December 4 (FTSE International; Datastream/ICV).

32 Dearlove, D., *Business the Bill Gates Way*, Capstone, Oxford, 1998.

33 Ibid.

34 *Fortune*, April 26, 1999.

35 *The Economist*, March 29, 1997.

36 www.GM.com.

37 *The World in 1999*, The Economist Publications, London, 1999.

38 *Fortune*, June 7, 1999.

39 Negroponte, N., *Being Digital.* Alfred A. Knopf, New York, 1995.

40 *Fortune*, June 7, 1999.

41 Davies, S. & Meyer, C., *Blur: The speed of change in the connected economy*, Capstone, Oxford, 1998.

42 *Bizniz*, March, 1998.

43 *Financial Times*, March 19, 1999.

44 *Financial World*, September–October, 1997.

45 Reich, R., *The Work of Nations: Preparing ourselves for 21st-century capitalism*, Simon & Schuster, New York, 1991.

46 *Svenska Dagbladet*, October 14, 1994.

47 CNC, *Screen Digest*, Eurostat.

48 *Business Week*, August 31, 1998.

49 *The Economist*, March, 29, 1997.

50 *Business Week*, August 25, 1997.

51 Ibid.

52 Ibid.

53 Rohwer, J., *Asia Rising: How the history's biggest middle class will change the world*, Nicholas Brealey, London, 1995.

54 Ibid.

55 Ibid.

56 *Business Week*, July 14, 1997.

57 *Business Week*, July 14, 1997.

58 Tapscott, D., *The Digital Economy: Promise and peril in the age of networked intelligence*, McGraw-Hill, New York, 1996.

59 "Strategies for Success in the Global Economy: An Interview with Rosabeth Moss Kanter", *Strategy & Leadership*, November/December, 1997.

60   *Business Week*, August 31, 1998.

61   *The Economist*, February 15, 1997.

62   *Financial Times*, December 8, 1998.

63   Kelly, K., *New Rules for the New Economy*, Penguin, Harmondsworth, Middlesex, 1998.

64   For a more detailed discussion of the cultural differences between these countries, see Hofstede, G., *Culture's Consequences*, Sage, Newbury Park, California, 1980.

65   *The Economist*, March, 29, 1997.

66   There are signs, perhaps, that the American perspective is changing. Lawrence Otis Graham, still best known for his 1992 article recounting his time spent as an undercover busboy in a Connecticut country club, argues that affirmative action and other diversity approaches have been rejected because they emphasize difference rather than the deeper characteristics that we all have in common. His latest book is called *Proversity*, a condensation of progressive diversity. Graham's message is that managers can – and must – recognize their bias and do something about it.

67   Taylor, J. & Wacker, W. (with Means, H.), *The 500 Year Delta: What happens after what comes next*, Harper Business, London, 1997.

68   Galbraith, J. K., *The New Industrial State*, Houghton Mifflin, Boston, Massachusetts, 1967.

69   Tapscott, D., *The Digital Economy: Promise and peril in the age of networked intelligence*, McGraw-Hill, New York, 1996.

70   Toffler, A., *The Third Wave*, Bantam, New York, 1980.

71   Knoke, W., *Bold New World: The essential road map to the twenty-first century*, Kodansha International, 1996.

72   For a discussion of lead customers and users, see Von Hippel, E., Lead Users: A source of novel product concepts, *Management Science*, Vol. 32, 1986.

73   Taylor, J. & Wacker, W. (with Means, H.), *The 500 Year Delta: What happens after what comes next*, Harper Business, London, 1997.

74   Granstrand, O. & Schölander, S., "Managing Innovation in Multi-technology Corporations", *Research Policy*, Vol. 18, 1989.

75   Frank, R. H. & Cook, P. J., *The Winner Take All Society*, The Free Press, New York, 1995.

76   *Fortune*, March 15, 1999.

4 Funky Inc.

1   Pascale, R., *Managing on the Edge*, Viking, New York, 1990.

2   *The Economist*, March 27, 1993.

3   Ibid.

4   Ibid.

5   Jager, R. M. & Ortiz, R., *In the Company of Giants: Candid conversations with the visionaries of the digital world*, McGraw-Hill, New York, 1997.

6   Smith, A., *An Inquiry Into the Nature and Causes of the Wealth of Nations*, The Modern Library, New York, 1776/1937.

7   Simon, H. A., *Administrative Behavior*, Macmillan, New York, 1947.

8   Ansoff, I., *Corporate Strategy*, McGraw-Hill, New York, 1965.

9 Tapscott, D., *The Digital Economy: Promise and peril in the age of networked intelligence*, McGraw-Hill, New York, 1996.

10 For the concept of core competence, see Hamel, G. & Prahalad, C. K., *Competing For the Future: Breakthrough strategies for seizing control of your industry and creating the markets of tomorrow*, Harvard Business School Press, Boston, Massachusetts, 1994. For the idea of core competents, see Hedlund, G. & Ridderstråle, J., in ed. McKern, B., *High Performance Global Corporations*, forthcoming, and Ridderstråle, J., *Global Innovation: Managing international innovation projects at ABB and Electrolux*, IIB, Stockholm, 1996.

11 If you are not laughing, re-read Chapter 3.

12 Hamel, G. & Prahalad, C. K., *Competing For the Future: Breakthrough strategies for seizing control of your industry and creating the markets of tomorrow*, Harvard Business School Press, Boston, Massachusetts, 1994.

13 Stewart, T. A., *Intellectual Capital: The new wealth of organizations*, Doubleday/Currency, New York, 1997.

14 *Fortune*, September 5, 1994.

15 Davies, S. & Meyer, C., *Blur: The speed of change in the connected economy*, Capstone, Oxford, 1998.

16 *Scanorama*, September, 1995.

17 *Fortune*, April 19, 1999.

18 Peters, Tom, *The Tom Peters Seminar*, Vintage Books, New York, 1994.

19 Ibid.

20 *Fortune*, February 15, 1999.

21 *Business Week*, November 3, 1997.

22 The example is borrowed from Taylor, J. & Wacker, W. (with Means, H.), *The 500 Year Delta: What happens after what comes next*, Harper Business, London, 1997.

23 *Fortune*, August 7 and August 21, 1995.

24 Ibid.

25 Pfeffer, J., *The Human Equation: Building profits by putting people first*, Harvard Business School Press, Boston, Massachusetts, 1998.

26 Koestler, A., *The Act of Creation*, Hutchinson & Company, London, 1964.

27 For the original metaphor, see Morgan, G., *Images of Organization*, Sage, Newbury Park, California, 1986 and Hedlund, G., "The Hypermodern MNC – A heterarchy?", *Human Resource Management*, spring, 1986.

28 *Business Week*, June 22, 1998.

29 Edvinsson, L. & Malone, M., *Intellectual Capital: The proven way to establish your company's real value by measuring its hidden brainpower*, Harper Business, London, 1997.

30 Michael Geoghegan of DuPont in Kao, J., *Jamming: The art & discipline of business creativity*, Harper Business, London, 1996.

31 *Fortune*, April 26, 1999.

32 Dearlove, D. & Crainer, S., *The Ultimate Book of Business Brands: Insight from the world's 50 greatest brands*, Capstone, Oxford, 1999.

33 Virgin Group literature.

34 *Financial Times*, December 8, 1998.

35 See Perlmutter, H. V., "The Tortuous Evolution of the Multinational Corporation", *Columbia Journal of World Business*, January–February, 1969, for the concept of ethnocentrism.

36 Trompenaars, F., *Riding the Waves of Culture*, Nicholas Brealey, London, 1993.

37 Ibid.

38 *Business Week*, August 25, 1997.

39 Kelly, K., *New Rules for the New Economy*, Viking, Harmondswoth, Middlesex, 1998.

40 The story was told to *Fortune* magazine, featuring Rubbermaid as the company of the year in 1994.

41 Speech by Assistant Professor Peter Hagström at the Advanced Management Program (Stockholm School of Economics), autumn, 1995.

42 Chandler, A. D., *Strategy and Structure*, MIT Press, Cambridge, Massachusetts, 1962.

43 Dearlove, D. & Crainer, S., *The Ultimate Book of Business Brands: Insight from the world's 50 greatest brands*, Capstone, Oxford, 1999.

44 Leonard-Barton, D., *The Wellsprings of Knowledge: Building and sustaining the sources of innovation*, Harvard Business School Press, Boston, Massachusetts, 1995.

45 For the theoretical argument, see Galbraith, J., *Designing Complex Organizations*, Addison-Wesley, Reading, Massachusetts, 1973 and *Organization Design*, Addison-Wesley, Reading, Massachusetts, 1977.

46 Kao, J., *Jamming: The art & discipline of business creativity*, Harper Business, London, 1996.

47 Stewart, T. A., *Intellectual Capital: The new wealth of organizations*, Doubleday/Currency, New York, 1997.

48 Fradette, M. & Michaud, S., *The Power of Corporate Kinetics: Create the self-adapting, self-renewing instant-action enterprise*, Simon & Schuster, New York, 1998.

49 *The Times*, 11 November, 1998, and www.barbie.com.

50 *Fortune*, September 28, 1998.

51 Peppers, D. & Rogers, M., *The One-to-one Future: Building relationships with one customer at a time*, Currency/Doubleday, New York, 1997.

52 Carlzon, J., *Riv Pyramiderna: En bok om den nya människan, chefen och ledaren*, Bonniers, 1985.

53 *Fortune*, September 28, 1998.

54 www.Razorfish.com.

55 The example is borrowed from Tapscott, D., *The Digital Economy: Promise and peril in the age of networked intelligence*, McGraw-Hill, New York, 1996.

56 Fradette, M. & Michaud, S., *The Power of Corporate Kinetics: Create the self-adapting, self-renewing instant-action enterprise*, Simon & Schuster, New York, 1998.

57 Kao, J., *Jamming: The art & discipline of business creativity*, Harper Business, London, 1996.

58 Janis, I., *Group Think*, 2nd ed., Houghton Mifflin, Boston, Massachusetts, 1982.

59 Ashby, W. R., *Design for a Brain*, John Wiley, New York, 1952.

60 *Fortune*, December 29, 1997.

61 *Fast Company*, December, 1998.

62 *Fortune*, January 12, 1998.

63 *Fortune*, March 17, 1997.

64 *Fortune*, September 29, 1997.

65 Our colleague Peter Hagström also talks about organizational tribes, though he gives the concept a slightly different meaning. Charles Handy uses the metaphor of organizations as membership communities.

66   Jung, C. G., ed. Staube de Laszlo, V., *The Basic Writings of C. G. Jung*, The Modern Library, New York, 1993.

67   *Fast Company*, August–September, 1996.

68   *Fortune*, January 16, 1995.

69   *Fortune*, May 2, 1994.

70   This idea was proposed to us by our colleague Peter Hagström.

71   Taylor, J. & Wacker, W. (with Means, H.), *The 500 Year Delta: What happens after what comes next,* Harper Business, London, 1997.

72   See Hedlund, G., in eds. Ghoshal, S. & Westney, E., *Organization Theory and the Multinational Corporation*, St Martin's Press, New York, 1993.

73   See Hedlund, G., "The Hypermodern MNC – A heterarchy?", *Human Resource Management*, spring, 1986 and Hedlund, G., in eds. Ghoshal, S. & Westney, E., *Organization Theory and the Multinational Corporation*, St Martin's Press, New York, 1993.

74   See Hedlund, G., in eds. Ghoshal, S. & Westney, E., *Organization Theory and the Multinational Corporation*, St Martin's Press, New York, 1993, Hedlund, G. & Ridderstråle, J., in eds. Toyne, B. & Nigh D., *International Business: An emerging vision*, University of South Carolina Press, 1997, and Hagström, P. & Hedlund, G. in eds. Chandler, A. D., Hagström, P. & Sölvell, Ö., *The Dynamic Firm: The role of technology, strategy, organization, and regions*, Oxford University Press, 1998, for the original three-dimensional model. Also see Nonaka, I. & Takeuchi, H., *The Knowledge Creating Company: How Japanese companies create the dynamics of innovation*, Oxford University Press, 1995, for a similar idea.

75   Hagström, P. & Hedlund, G. in eds. Chandler, A. D., Hagström, P. & Sölvell, Ö., *The Dynamic Firm: The role of technology, strategy, organization, and regions*, Oxford University Press, 1998.

76   *Financial Times*, March 1, 1999.

77   Naisbitt, J., in ed. Gibson, R., *Rethinking the Future*, Nicholas Brealey, London, 1997.

78   *Fast Company*, September, 1998.

79   Nicholson, N., How hardwired is human behavior?, *Harvard Business Review*, July/August, 1998.

80   Peters, T., *The Tom Peters Seminar: Crazy times call for crazy organizations*, Macmillan, London, 1994.

81   *Fortune*, January 11, 1999.

82   *Financial Times*, May 11, 1994.

83   Nonaka, I., "Toward Middle-up-down Management: Accelerating information creation", *Sloan Management Review*, spring, 1988.

84   *Fortune*, September 5, 1994.

85   Hedlund, G., "The Intensity and Extensity of Knowledge and the Multinational Corporation as a Nearly Recomposable System (NRS)", *Management International Review*, Special Issue, 1, 1999.

86   Casti, J. L., *Complexification: Explaining a paradoxical world through the science of surprise*, Harper Perennial, London, 1994.

87   Referred to in Kelly, Kevin, *Out of Control*, Fourth Estate, London, 1994.

88   *Fortune*, October 3, 1994.

89   *Fortune*, May 29, 1995.

90 Handy, C., *The Empty Raincoat: Making sense of the future*, Hutchinson, London, 1995.

5 Funky U

1   *Fast Company*, November, 1998.
2   Handy, C., *The Empty Raincoat: Making sense of the future*, Hutchinson, London, 1994.
3   *Fortune*, October 27, 1998.
4   Bartlett, C. A. & Ghoshal, S., *Managing Across Borders: The transnational solution*, Hutchinson, London, 1989.
5   The following examples are borrowed from Collins, J. C. & Porras, J. I., *Built to Last: Successful habits of visionary companies*, Harper Business, London, 1994.
6   The Drucker Foundation, *The Organization of the Future*, Jossey-Bass, San Francisco, 1996.
7   *Fast Company*, December, 1998.
8   Said by Yogen K. Dalal in *Business Week*, August 25, 1997.
9   Crainer, S., *The 75 Greatest Management Decisions*, AMACOM, New York, 1999.
10 Lowe, J., *Jack Welch Speaks*, John Wiley, New York, 1998.
11 Welch, J., "Shun the incremental", *Financier*, July, 1984.
12 Interview, January, 1994.
13 Kleiner, K., "Beware experts carrying stigmas", *New Scientist*, 21 October, 1995.
14 Crainer, S., *The Ultimate Book of Business Quotations*, AMACOM, New York, 1998.
15 *Fortune*, May 15, 1995.
16 Crainer, S., *The 75 Greatest Management Decisions*, AMACOM, New York, 1999.
17 Peters, T., *The Circle of Innovation: You can't shrink your way to greatness*, Hodder & Stoughton, London, 1997.
18 Smith, A., *An Inquiry into the Nature and the Causes of the Wealth of Nations*, The Modern Library, New York, 1776/1937.
19 *Fortune*, September 29, 1997.
20 Davies, S. & Botkin, J., *The Monsters Under the Bed: How business is mastering the opportunity of knowledge for profit*, Simon & Schuster, New York, 1994.
21 Dearlove, D. & Crainer, S., *Gravy Training*, Jossey-Bass, San Francisco, 1999.
22 Ibid.
23 Ibid.
24 Ibid.
25 Ibid.
26 *Fortune*, January 11, 1999.
27 *Fast Company*, August, 1998.
28 *Fast Company*, January, 1999.
29 Hamel, G., Foreword to *Financial Times Handbook of Management*, FT/Pitman, London, 1995.
30 Crainer, S., *Business the Jack Welch Way*, AMACOM, New York, 1999.
31 "Is loyalty really dead?", *Human Resources*, June, 1999.
32 Ibid.
33 *Business Week*, October 13, 1997.

34 *Fast Company*, June, 1999.

35 *Fortune*, July 20, 1998.

36 Tom Peters Seminar, London, The Economist Intelligence Unit, 1993.

37 Carlsson, S., *Executive Behaviour*, Stockholm, Strömbergs, 1951.

38 *Fortune*, May 10, 1999.

6 Feeling funky

1   Interview, *MTC Nytt*, 1994.

2   *Financial Times*, November 16, 1998.

3   Kelleher, Herb, "A culture of commitment, *Leader to Leader*", spring, 1997.

4   Jager, R. M. & Ortiz, R., *In the Company of Giants: Candid conversations with the visionaries of the digital world*, McGraw-Hill, New York, 1997.

5   *Business Week*, 30 March, 1998.

6   Peters, Tom, *The Pursuit of Wow: Every person's guide to topsy-turvy times*, Vintage, New York, 1994.

7   Dearlove, D. & Crainer, S., *The Ultimate Book of Brands: Insights from the world's 50 greatest brands*, Capstone, Oxford, 1999.

8   *Fast Company*, June–July, 1998.

9   *Fortune*, May 24, 1999.

10 *Fortune*, June 23, 1997.

11 *Time* magazine, December 7, 1998.

12 *Fortune*, 12 January 1998.

CREDITS FOR PHOTOS AND ILLUSTRATIONS

Gunnar Hedlund Award
Womax AB, Stockholm

Karl Marx
Pressens Bild, Stockholm

Berlin wall
Gerard Malie/Pressens Bild, Stockholm

Airport arrival/departure
Frank Chmura/Tiofoto, Stockholm

Stockholm School of Economics
Konny Domnauer

Cheetah
Manoj Shah/Tony Stone Images, Stockholm

Dalai Lama
Ralph Crane/IMS Bildbyrå, Stockholm

White water rafting
Claes Grundsten/Bildhuset, Stockholm

Bazaar
Ulf Sjöstedt/Tiofoto, Stockholm

Reinvent yourself
Womax AB, Stockholm

Tripp Trapp children's chair
Stokke, Norway

TV watcher
Mats Sandelin/Pressens Bild, Stockholm

Subway in Tokyo, Japan
IMS Bildbyrå/Stockholm

Supermarket
Alexander Farnsworth/Pressens Bild, Stockholm

Watch
Bo K. Englbrecht, Stockholm

Brain scan
Roy Ooms/Pressens Bild, Stockholm

Factory
Hulton Getty/Tony Stone Images, Stockholm

Day and Night, 1938
©1999 M.C. Escher/Cordon Art B.V. Baarn, Holland

Hell's angels
Bob Skinner/Pressens Bild, Stockholm

The Pope and biker
Bo K. Englbrecht, Stockholm
Pope Pressens Bild, Stockholm
Biker Torleif Svensson/Tiofoto, Stockholm

Building being demolished
Fred Charles/Tony Stone Images, Stockholm

Flags
Frank Chmura/Tiofoto, Stockholm

Branson in wedding dress
Kevin Lamarque/Pressens Bild, Stockholm

Spaghetti
AB Cerealia, Stockholm

Marathon
Rickard Forsberg, Stockholm Marathon, Stockholm

Pioneer F/G
Nasa Photographic Public Sales, Maryland, USA

Jesus
Rita Lönnroth/IMS Bildbyrå, Stockholm

Alfred Nobel
The Nobel Foundation, Stockholm

American Post Art, 1964
©Roy Lichtenstein/BUS 1999, Modern Museum, Stockholm

Linda Lampenius
Jussi Nukari/Pressens Bild, Stockholm

Me Inc.
Kenneth Andersson, Stockholm

Juggler
Denny Lorentzen/Pressens Bild, Stockholm

Organization
Thomas Wester/Bildhuset, Stockholm

Alessi, toilet brush
Bo K. Englbrecht, Stockholm

Buddha
Thia Konig/Tony Stone Images, Stockholm

Sushi
Lennart Durehed/IMS Bildbyrå, Stockholm

Wedding cake
Peter Dazeley/Tony Stone Images, Stockholm

Trapped in cage
Eva Redhe